Fantastic Art And The Creative Process

Volume 1

ViSiOn
ILLUSTRATED

First Printing: 2016

ISBN: 13: 978-1503108264

Because of the dynamic nature of the Internet, any web addresses or links contained in this book may have changed
since publication and may no longer be valid. The views expressed in this work are solely those of the author and do
not necessarily reflect the views of the publisher, and the publisher hereby disclaims any responsibility for them.

Cover art from left to right:
Scholar - Robinson Crusoe by Donato Giancola
Redeem The Knight: Blood Ties by Hugo Bravo
The Gathering Storm by Patrick Jones
The Rescuer by Petar Meseldzija

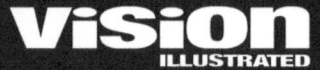 www.visionillustrated.com

Fantastic Art And The Creative Process

Volume 1

ViSiON
ILLUSTRATED

Edited by
HUGO BRAVO

art by Hugo Bravo

Fantastic Art And The Creative Process

Volume 1

ViSiON
ILLUSTRATED

Contributing Artists Index

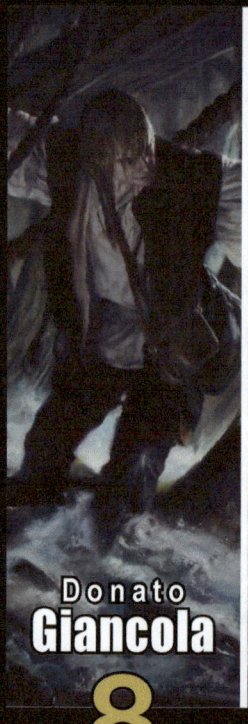

Donato
Giancola
8

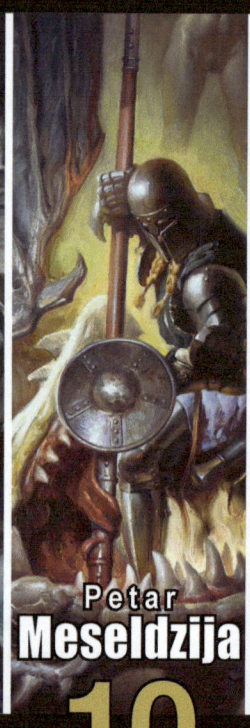

Petar
Meseldzija
10

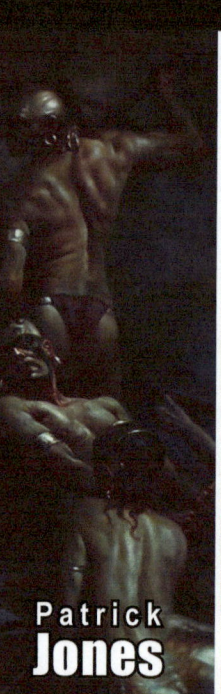
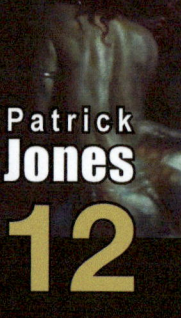

Patrick
Jones
12

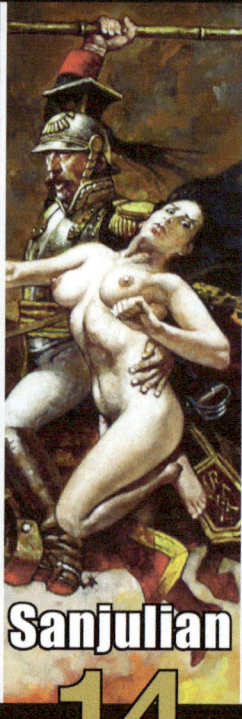

Sanjulian
14

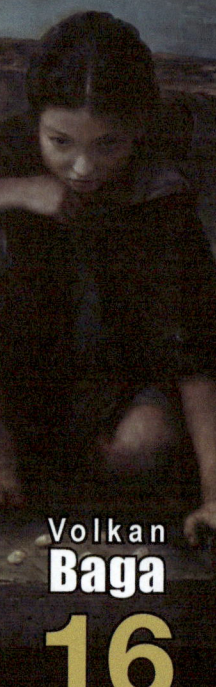

Volkan
Baga
16

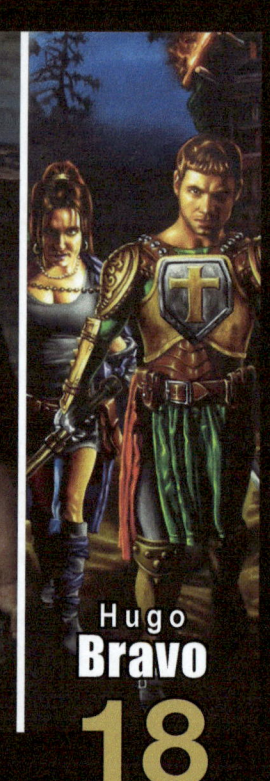

Hugo
Bravo
18

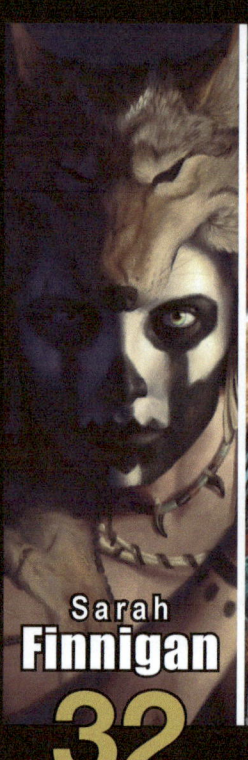

Sarah
Finnigan
32

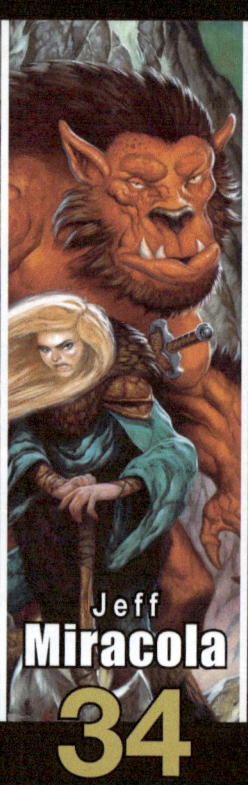

Jeff
Miracola
34

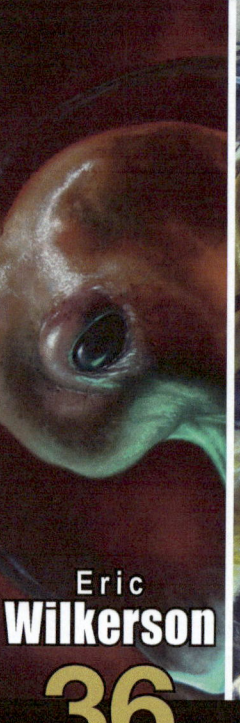

Eric
Wilkerson
36

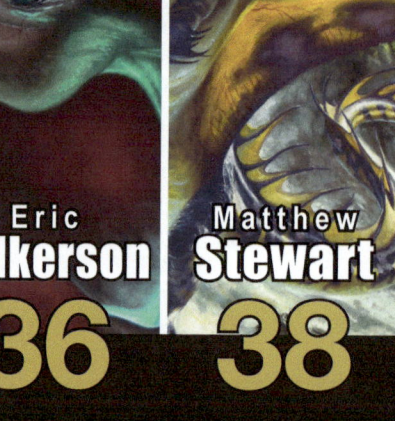

Matthew
Stewart
38

Lindsey
Look
40

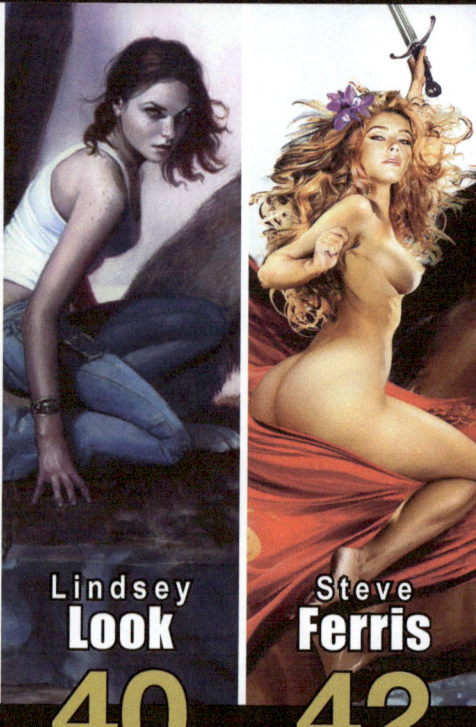

Steve
Ferris
42

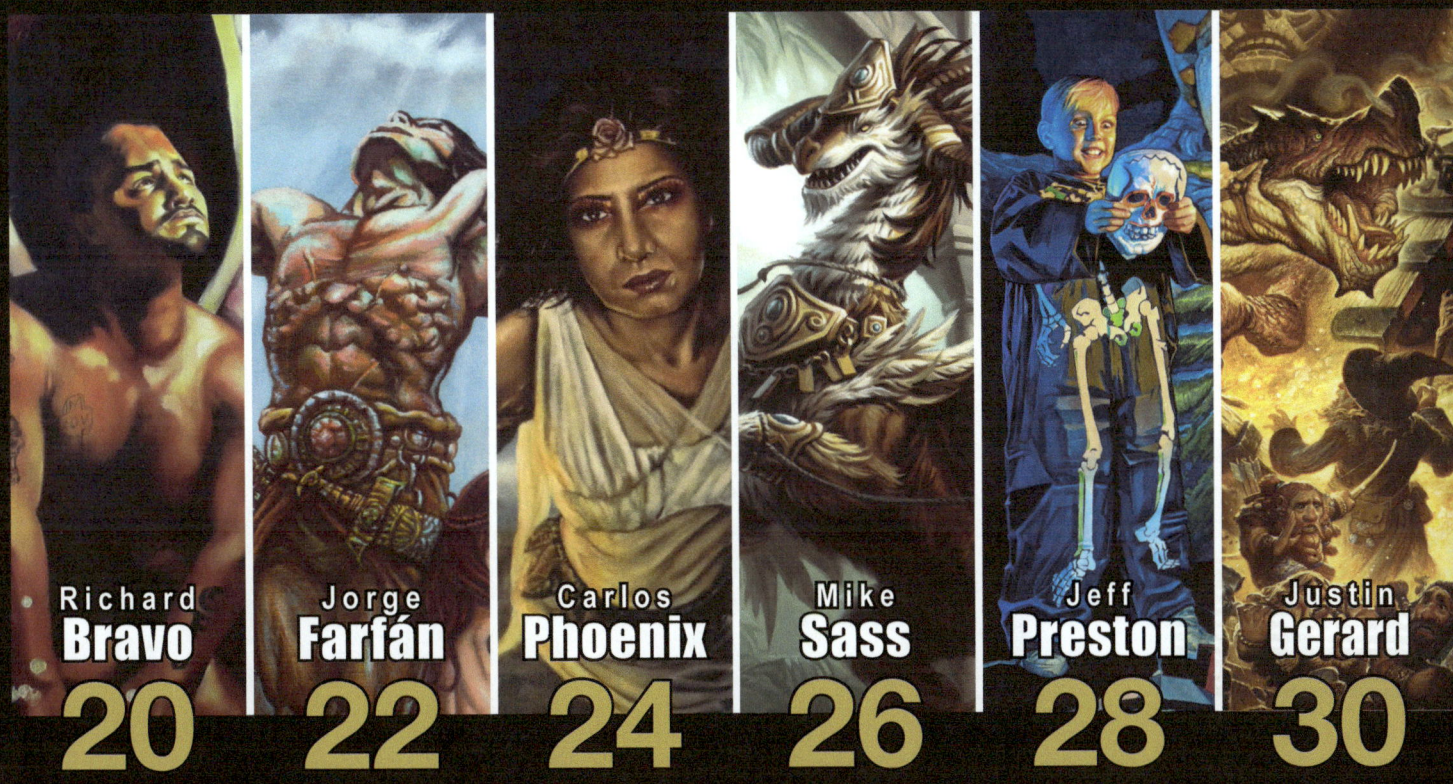

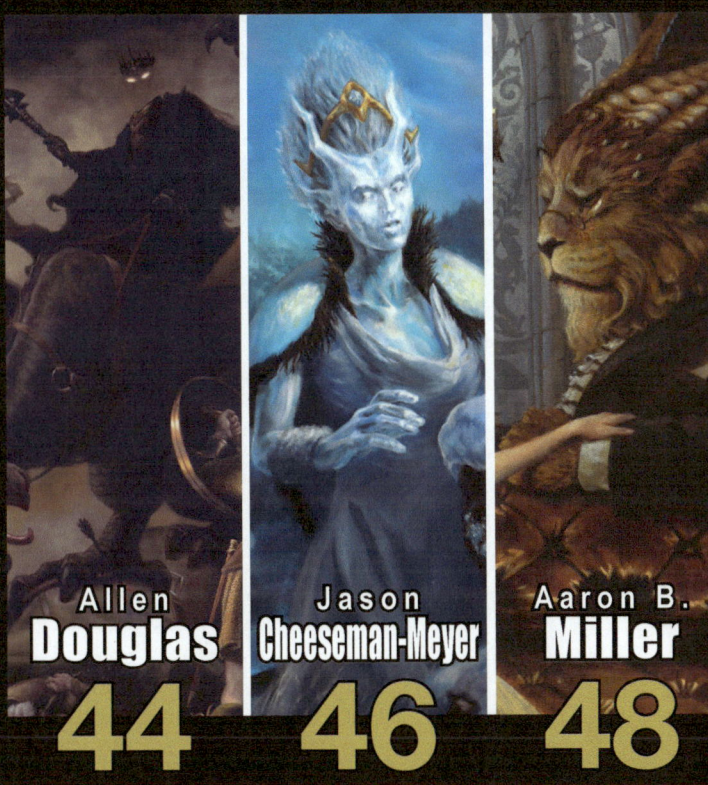

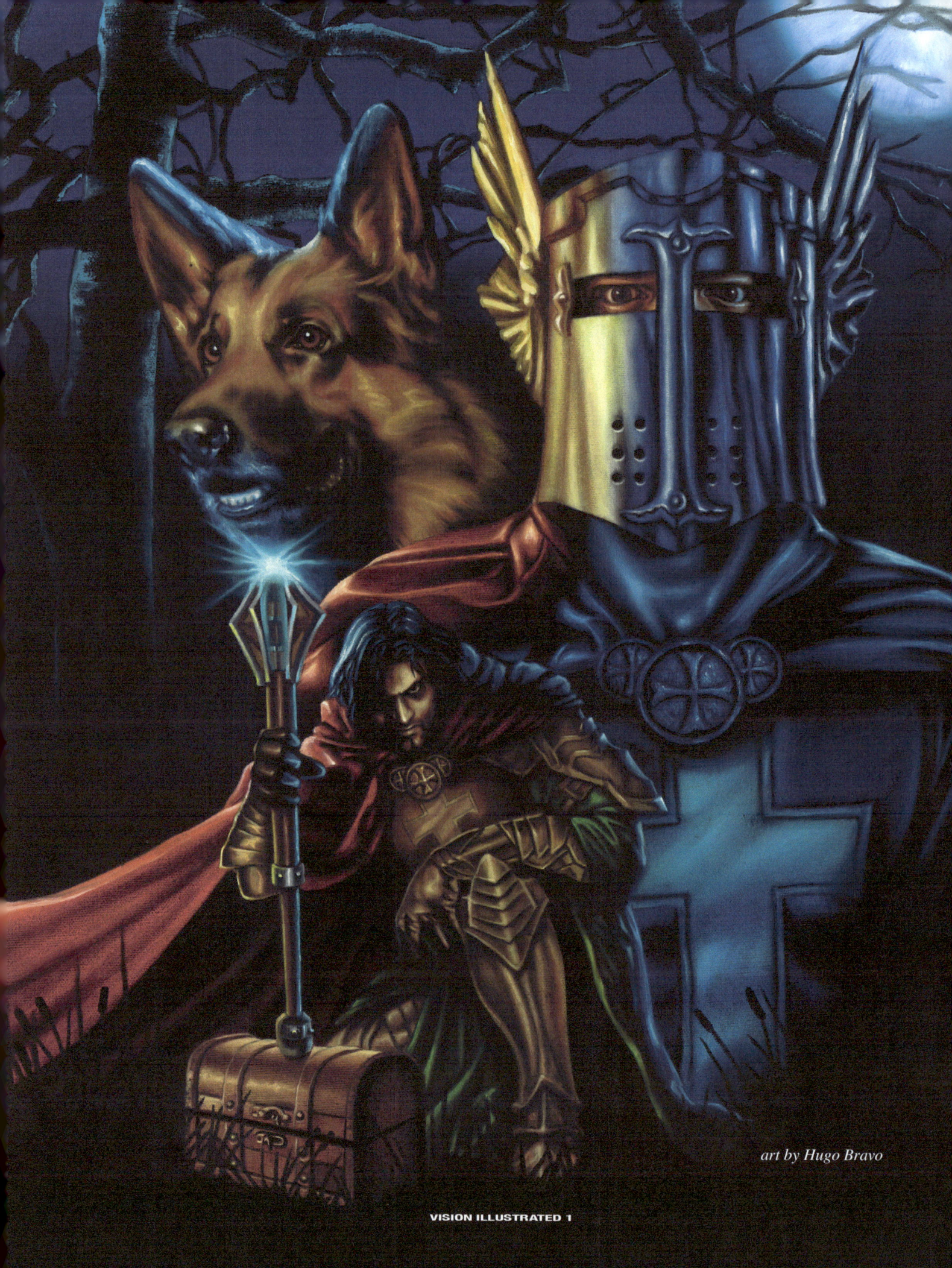

art by Hugo Bravo

Forward

by Hugo Bravo

Vision Illustrated is the answer to the questions I along with many artists and art fans have after looking through art annuals and compilation books: "How did they do it?" How did the artists create these masterpieces"?

Most art annuals and compilation books focus on the final work of art, with no insight as to what steps the artist took to get there. So I thought what if I created a book where the artists can take the reader on that journey with them. "Vision Illustrated" is that book.

Great idea but now what?

I am an illustrator, working in the field since '92. I have experience working for publishers but never published anything of my own. I knew the learning curve for publishing a book was high, but I dove right in. Seeking information from many sources like the internet, clients and fellow artists, I soon became aware that is was not going to be easy and it will take some time.

The first big challenge was how and where do I find the artists to feature in the book? The first idea that came to mind was to follow the process that other art annual and compilation books use: announce a call for entries, charge artists for submitting work for a jury to judge and select the winners for inclusion in the book.

After thinking it over, I felt that approach would be overwhelming for one person to handle. I would have to deal with hundreds of entries, judge them all myself or find a jury to do it.
What to do? What to do?

So I came up with plan B.

Why not email exclusive invitations to artists that inspire me and whose work I admire. While putting the list together, I wondered what were the chances that these well known artists would want to be in my book. I mean the top names on my list already have published books of their own and some even have "how to" DVDs.

But you know what, I did not let that discourage me from trying to get them. I wrote the intro email and took a deep breath and hit "send". My first email went out to science fiction and fantasy illustrator Donato Giancola. Days went by with no reply. Donato is an illustrator in high demand so I knew I had to be patient. Then one day it happened, I recieved the reply I was hoping for, a big "yes". With this new inspiration I sent the rest of the emails to the remaining artists on my list. Not all of them said "yes" or even replied, but there were enough "yeses" for me to create the book as I envisioned. I am proud to say you now hold that "vision".

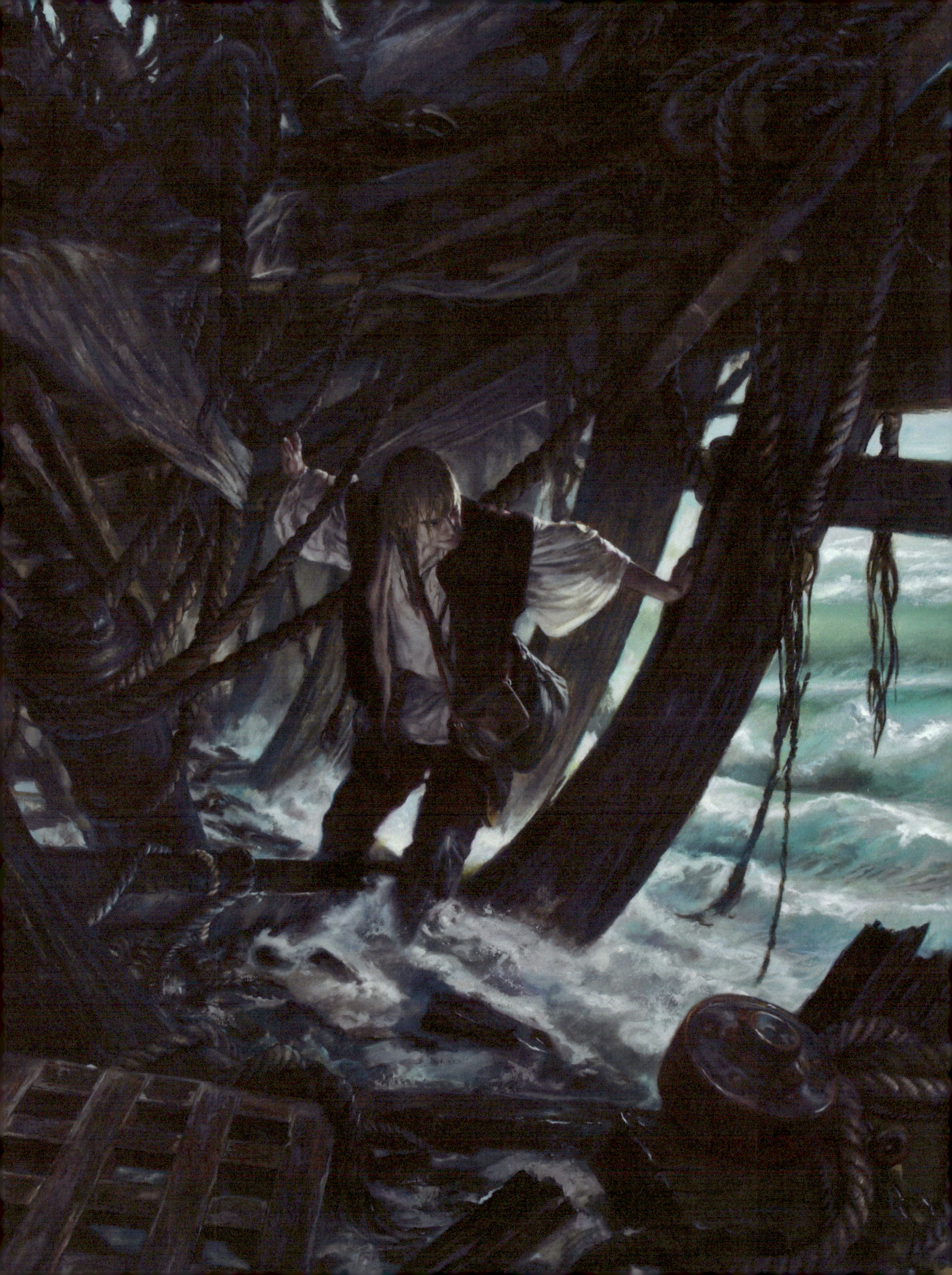

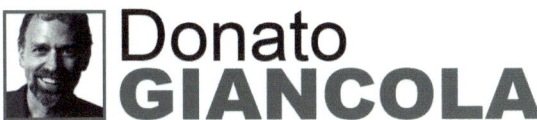

Donato GIANCOLA

Website: www.donatoart.com
Email: donato@donatoart.com
Title: Scholar - Robinson Crusoe
Art: Oil on panel 36"x48"
Portrait photo by: Greg Preston

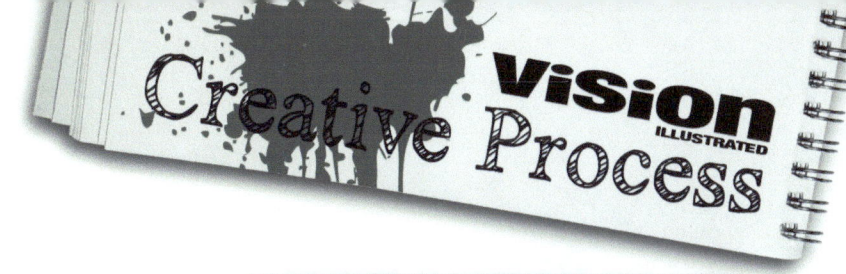

Creative Process
Vision ILLUSTRATED

1 Thumbnail Sketches

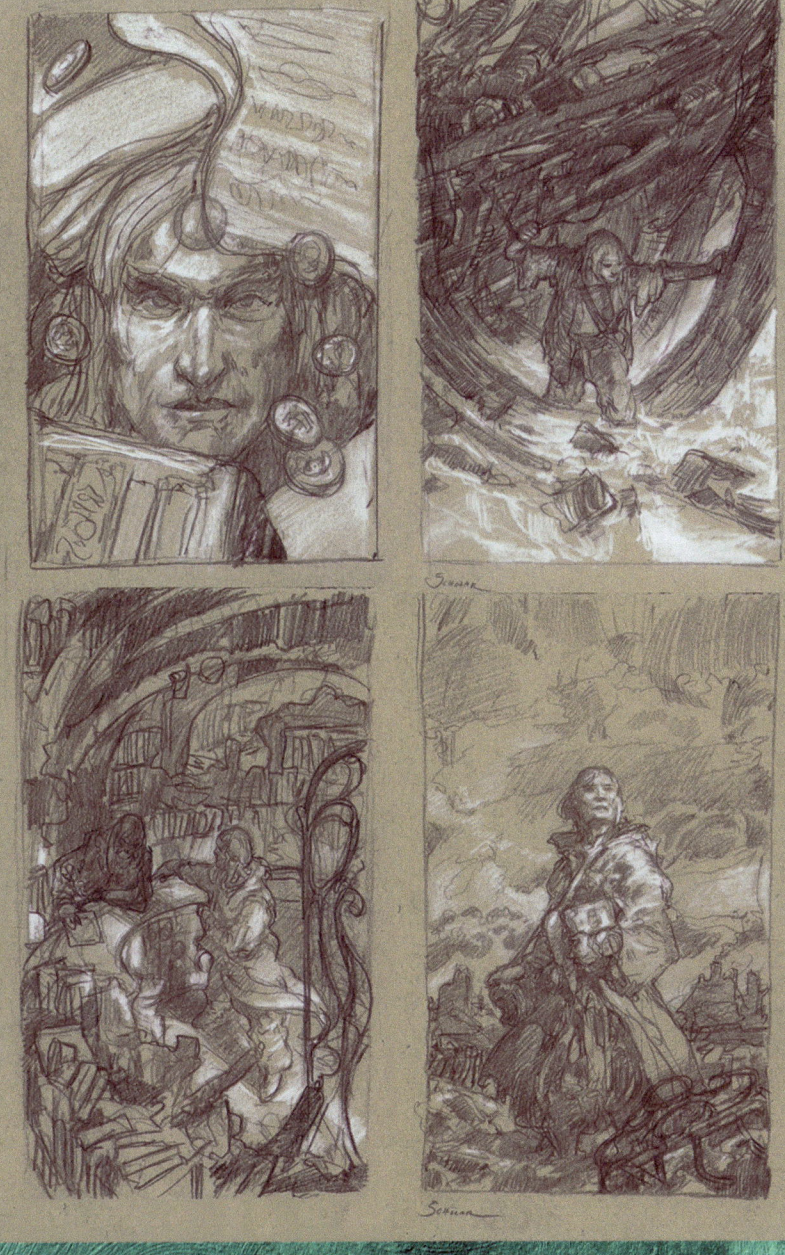

2 Photo Reference

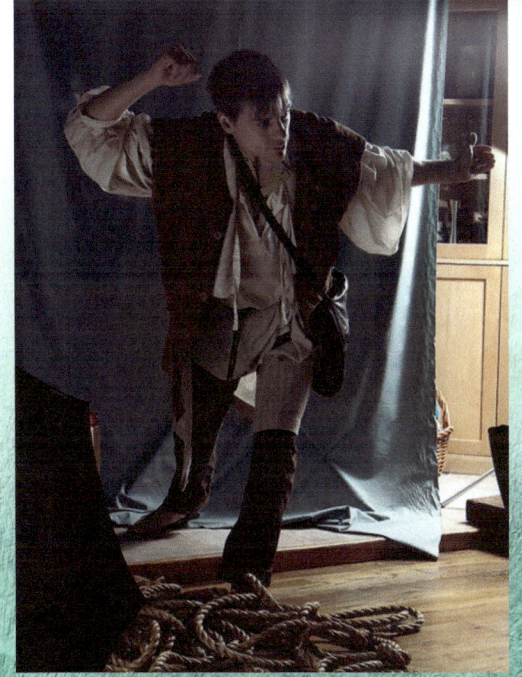

3 Final Drawing

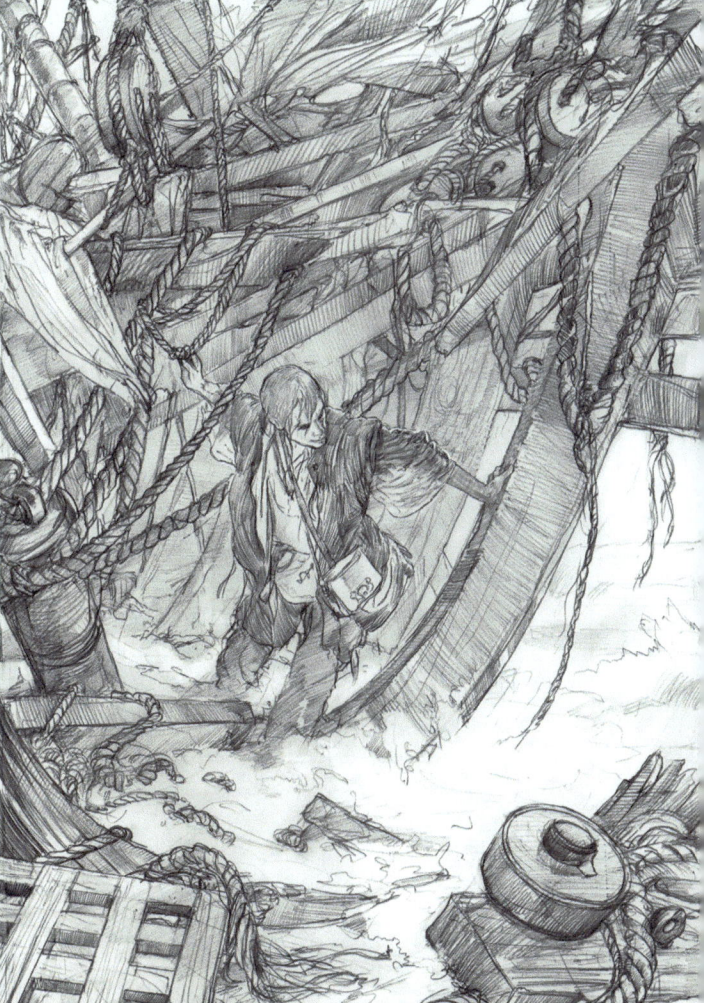

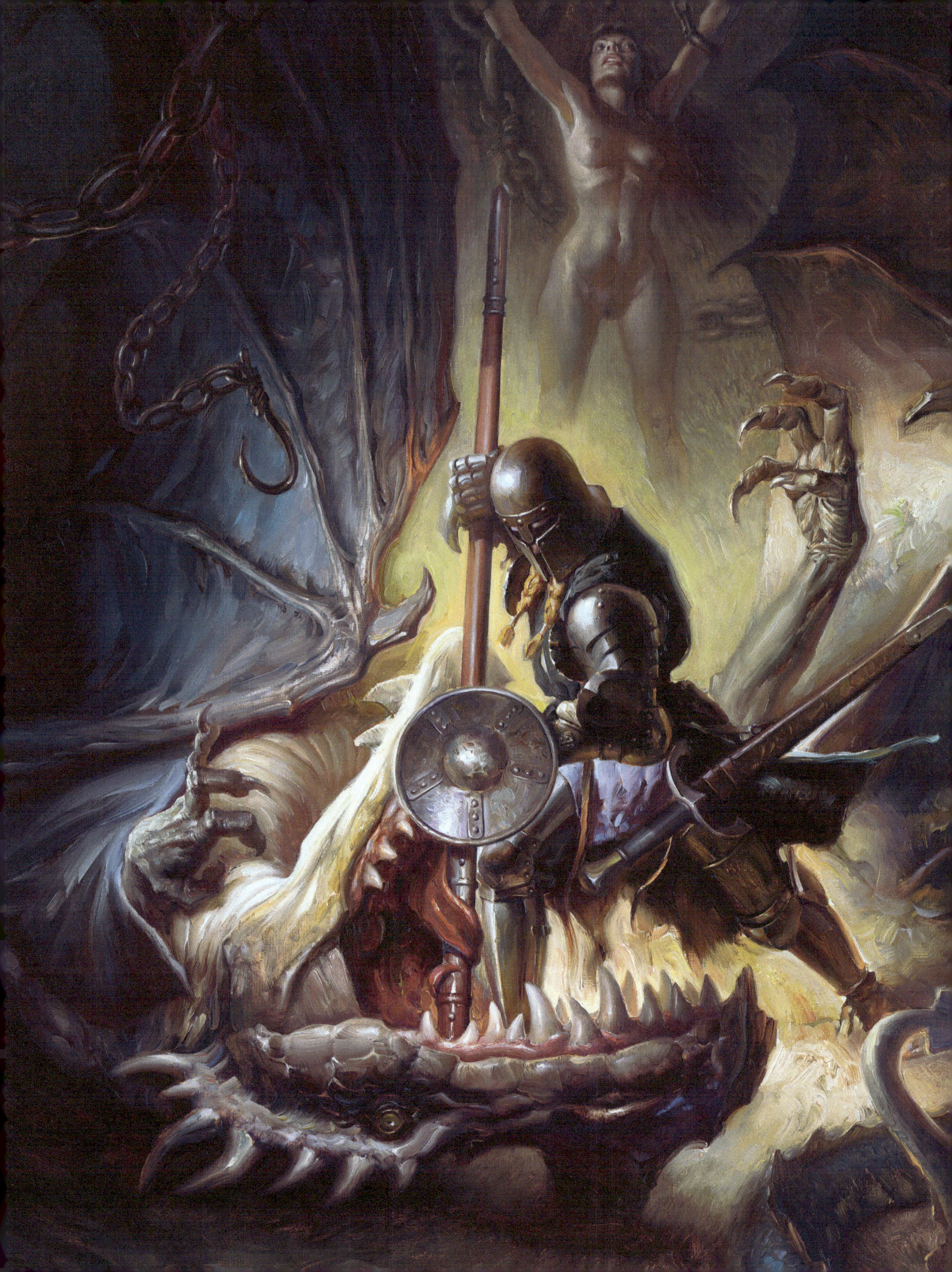

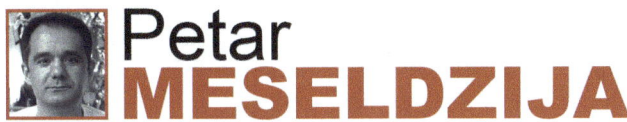

Petar MESELDZIJA

Website: www.petarmeseldzijaart.com
Email: petarmeseldzija@planet.nl
Blog: http://petarmeseldzija.blogspot.nl/
Title: The Rescuer
Art: Oil on Masonite, 60x43 cm / 23,6x16,9 inch
2011 (Private collection)

1 Thumbnail Sketches

2 Photo Reference

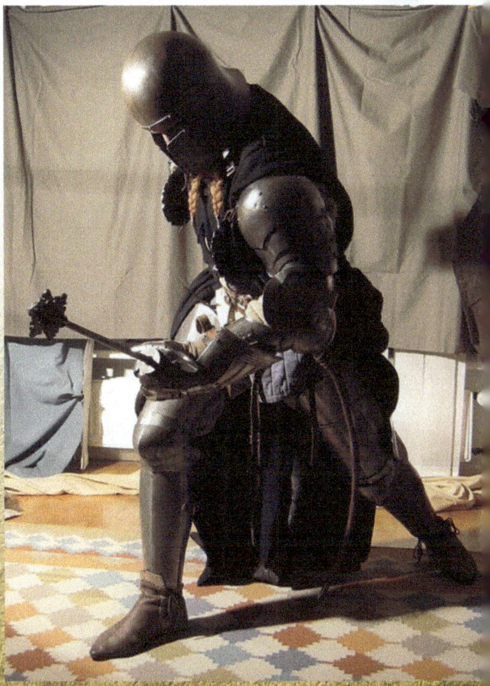

3 Final Drawing

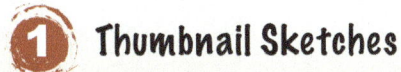

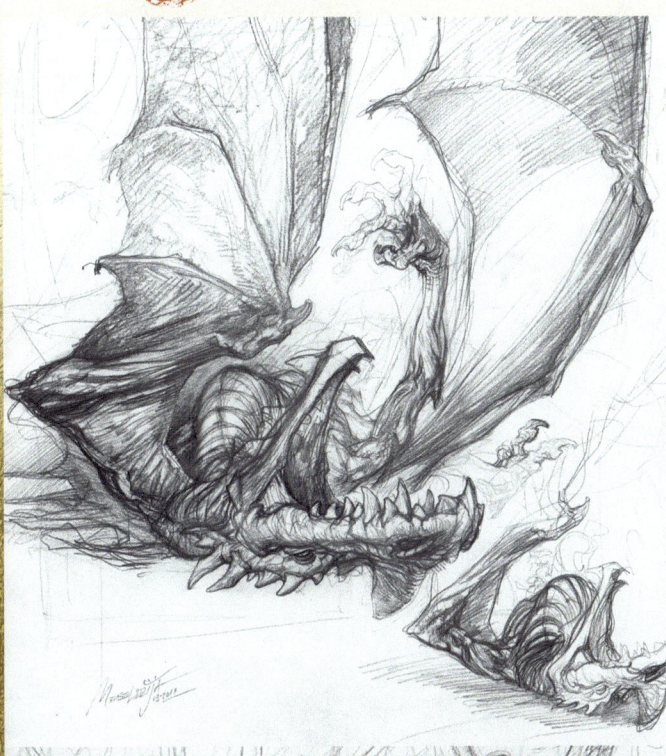

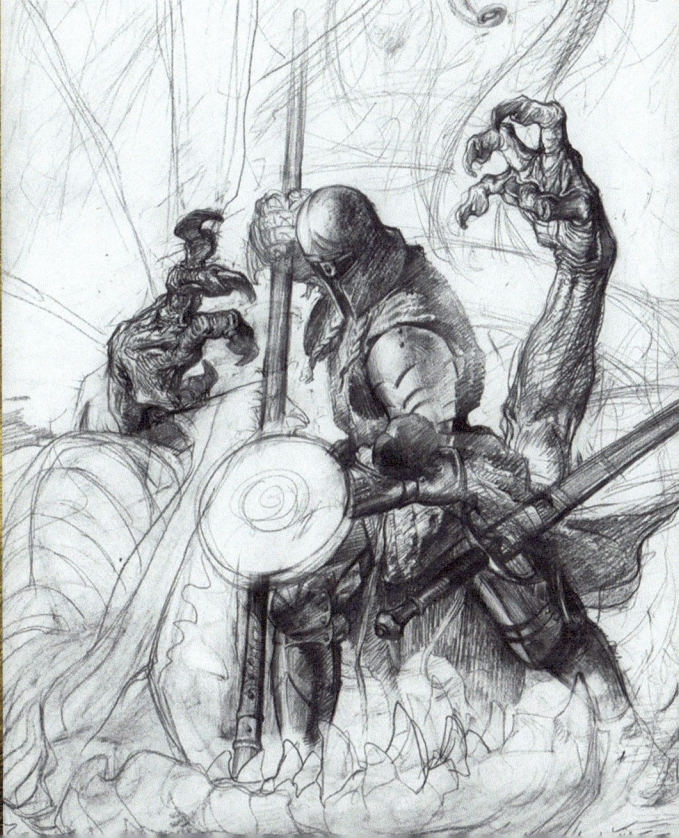

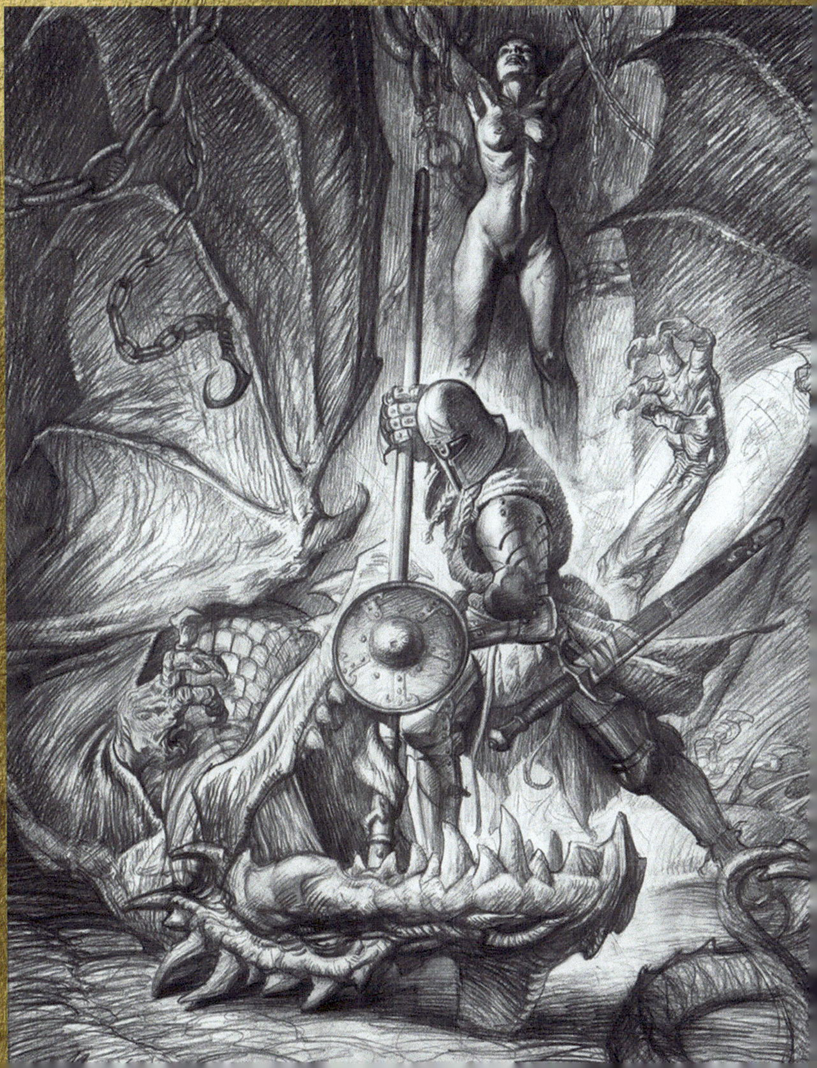

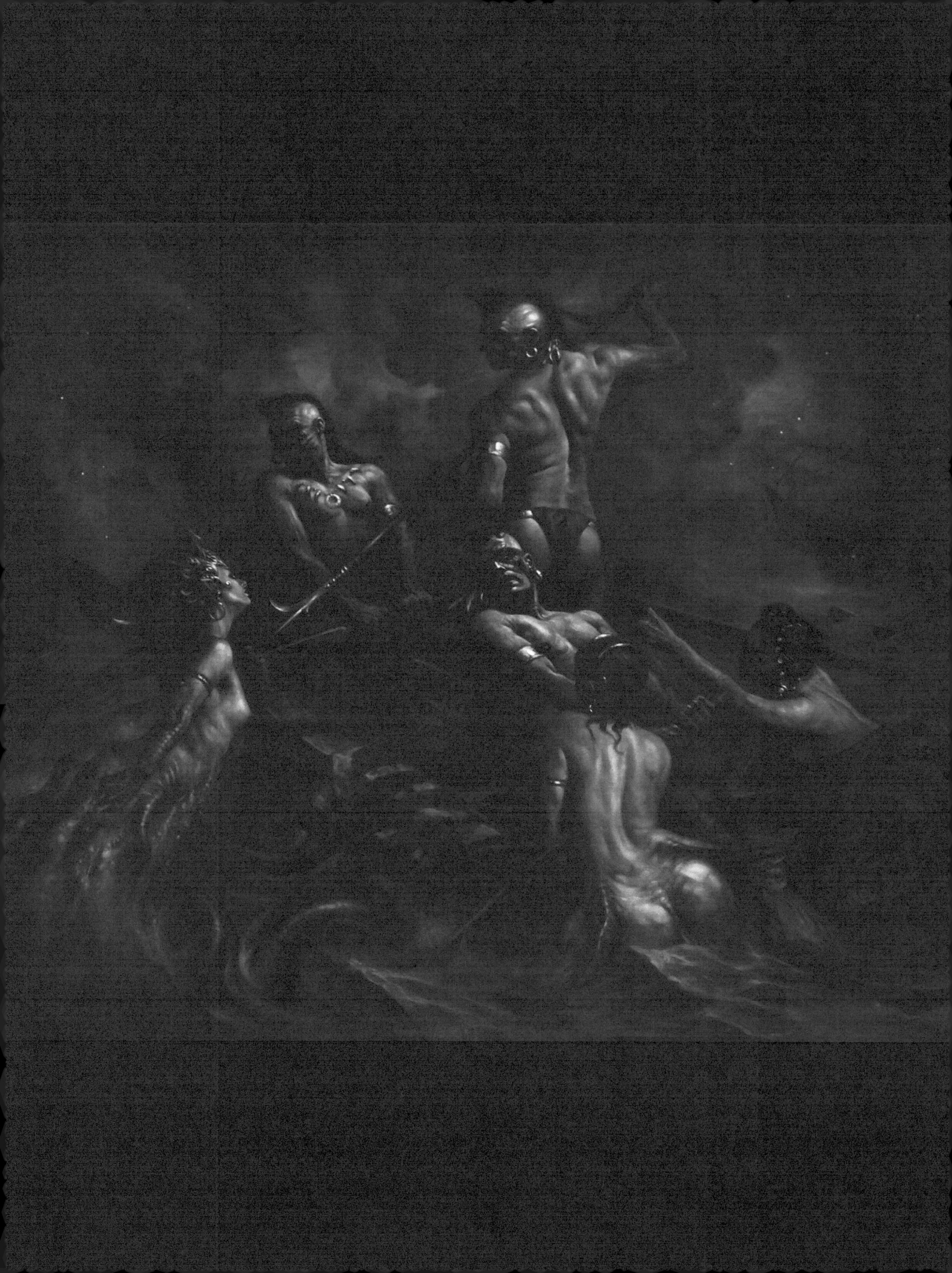

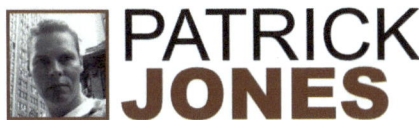

PATRICK JONES

Website: www.pjartworks.com
Title: The Gathering Storm
Art: Oil on board 22" x 28"

① Thumbnail Sketches

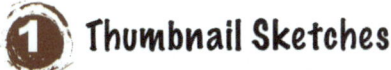

BOSTON
HARBOUR

CLIPPER

FLOATING
TEA

TEA

BRITISH FLAG

MOHAWK INDIAN
WITH BOAT HOOK

SHIP IN HARBOUR
MIST

LARGE
DRAMATIC
WAVES

WILD
HAIR

MERMAID
TIPPING BOAT

SONS OF LIBERTY HEADING
TOWARD CLIPPER

UNION JACK   1773 DATE ON SIDE OF
BOAT

SEA SERPENT

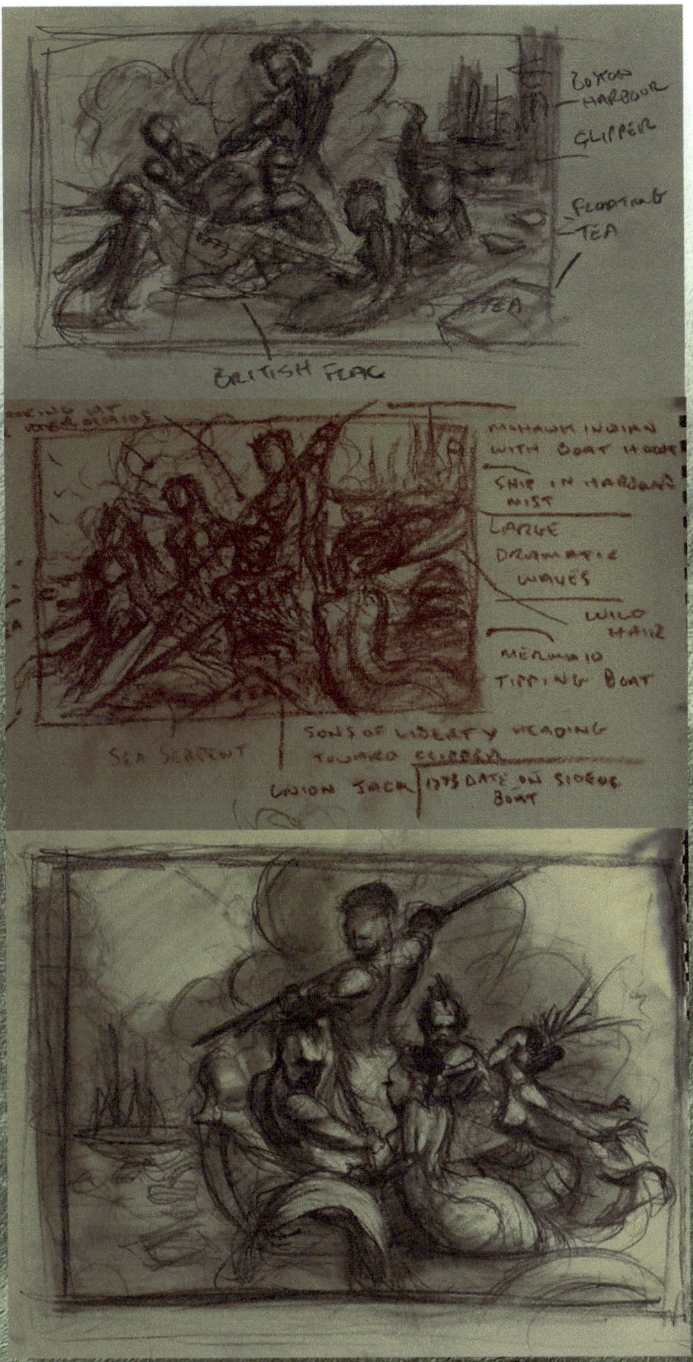

② Color Study

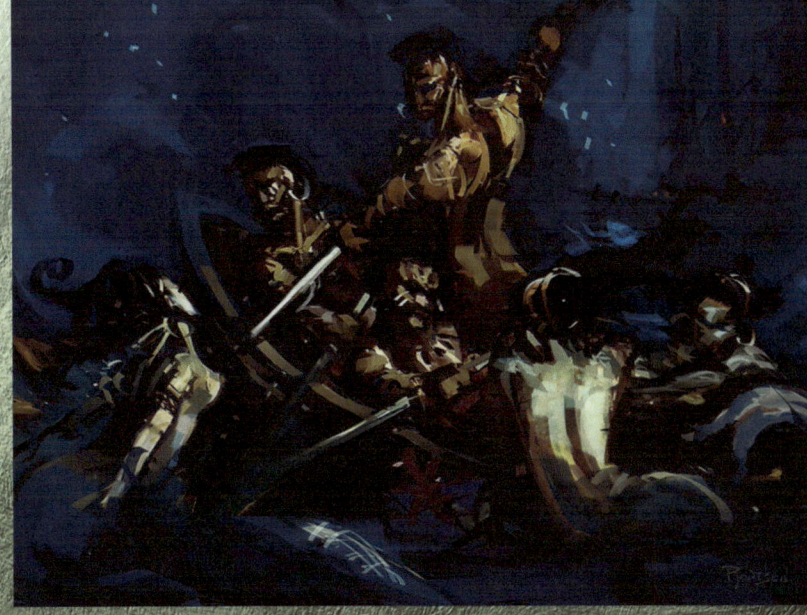

③ Final Drawing

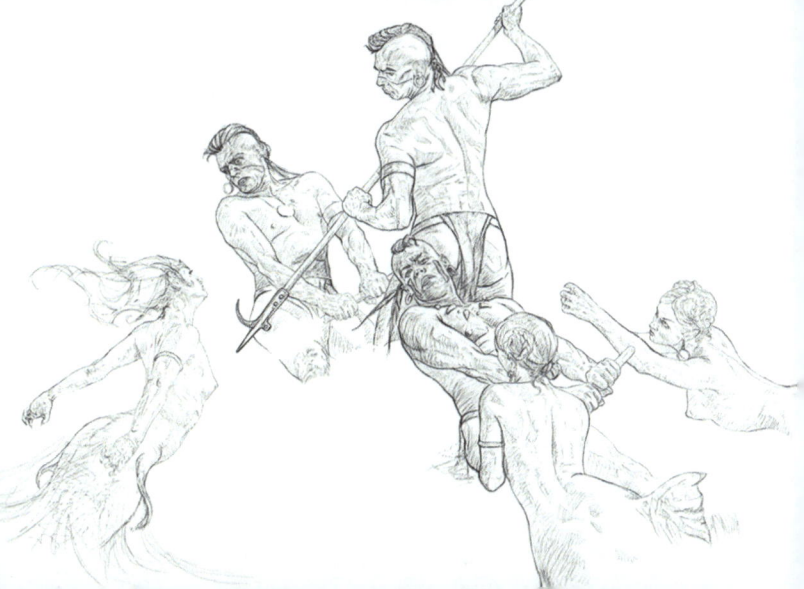

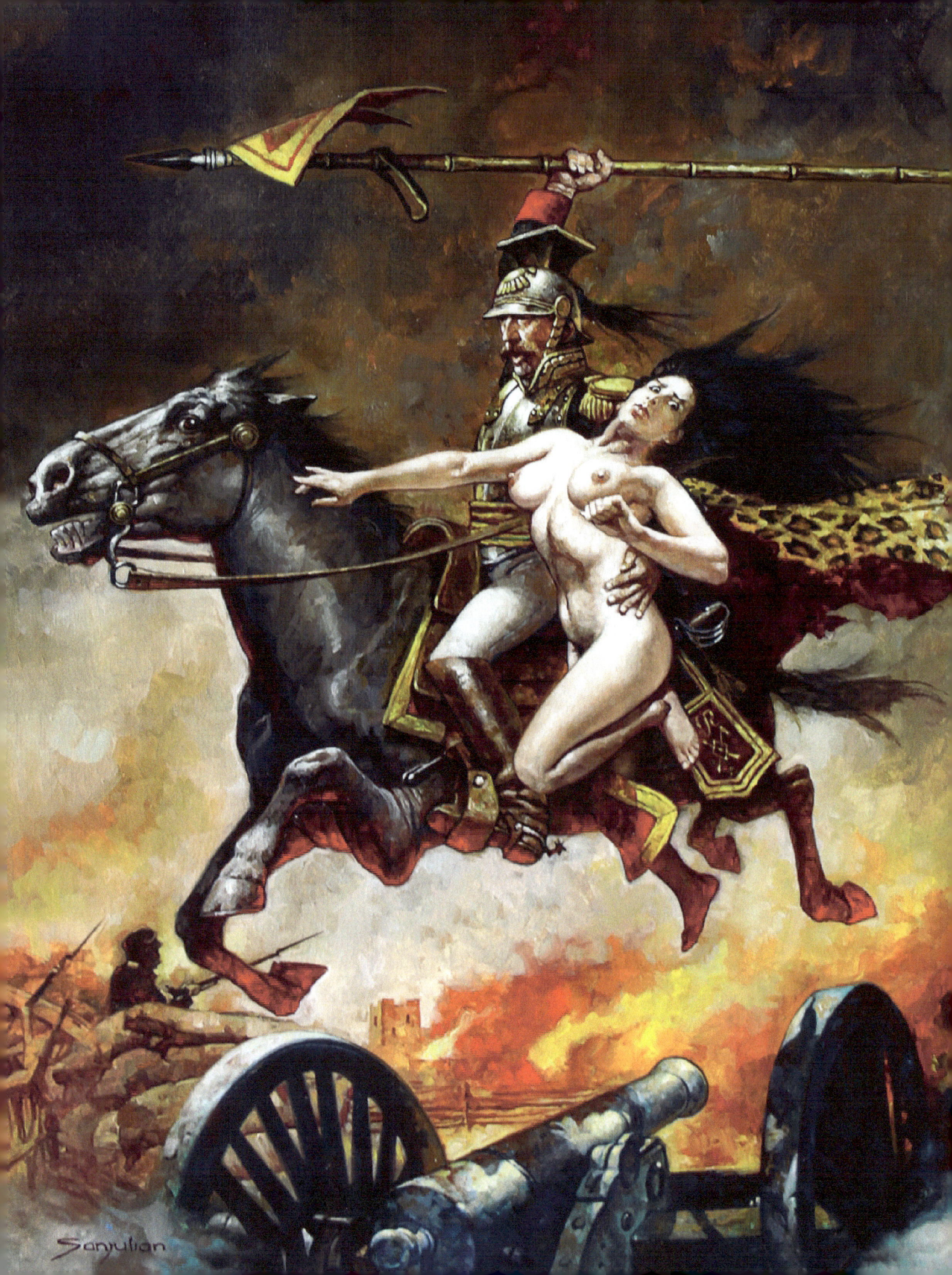

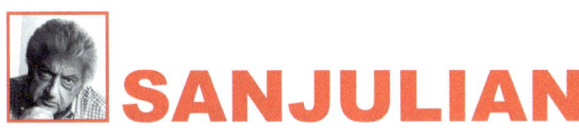

SANJULIAN

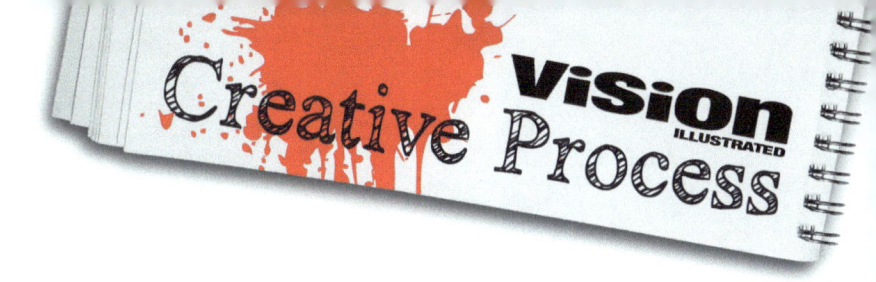

Website: www.sanjulian.info
Email: sanjulian25@yahoo.es
Title: Flashman
Art: Oils on linen 53x40 cm / 20,8x15,7 inch

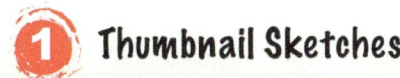

1 Thumbnail Sketches

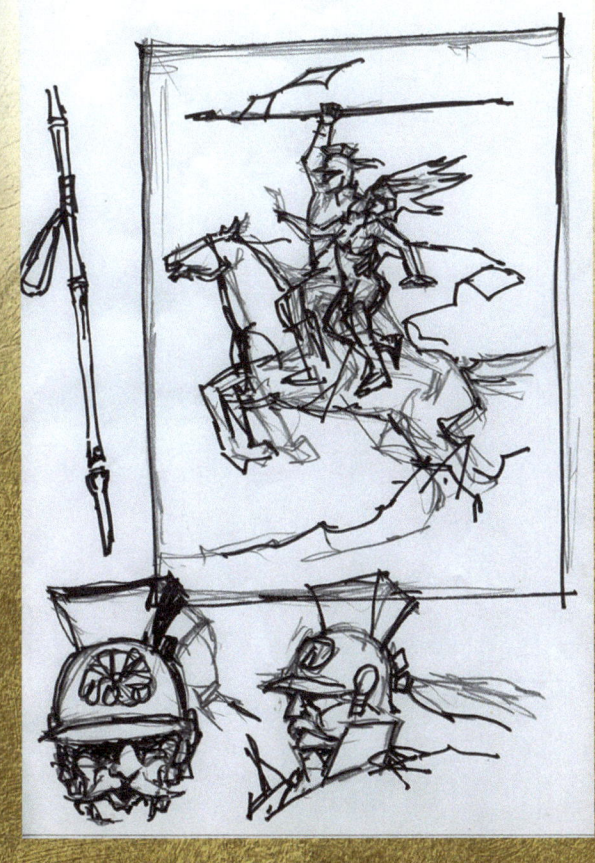

2 Final Drawing

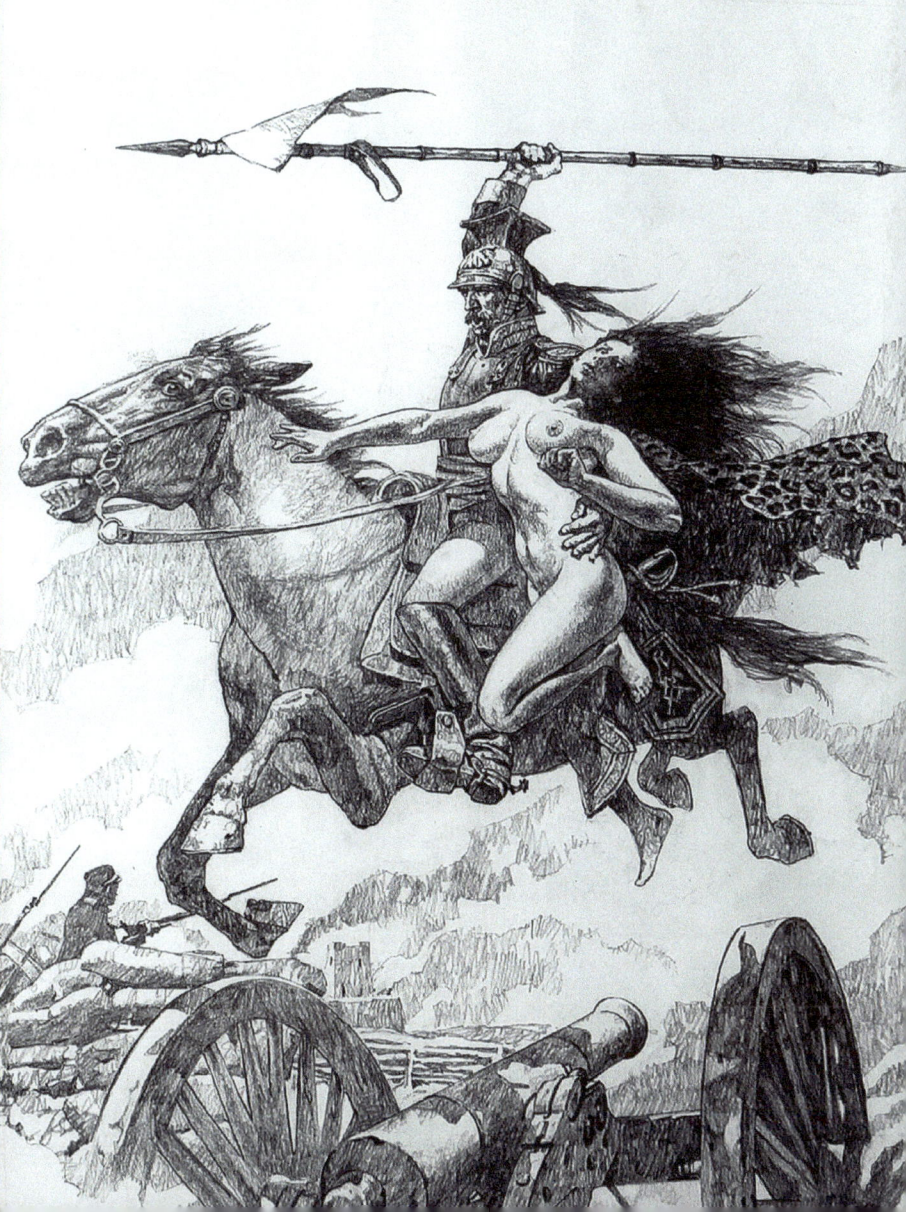

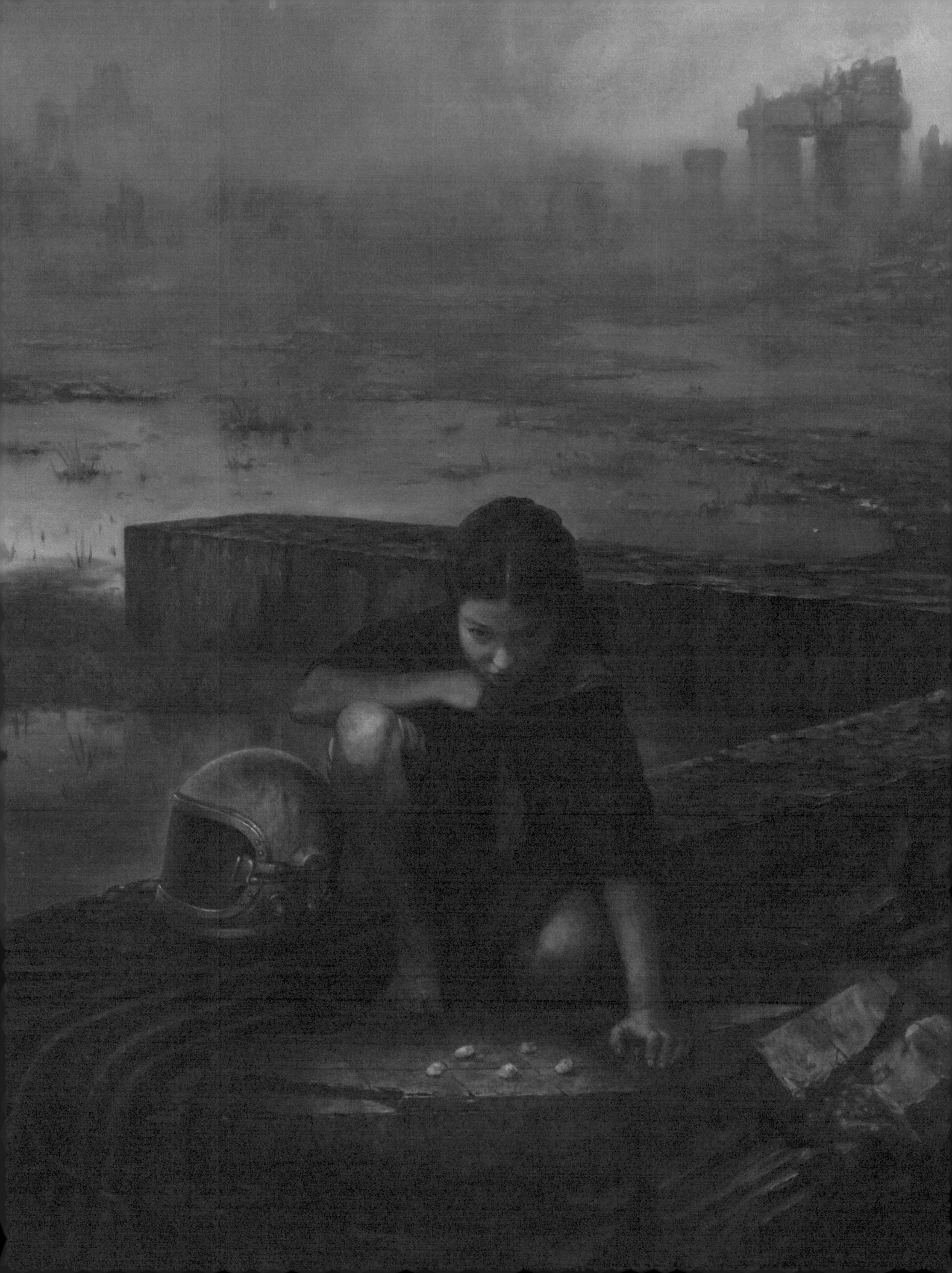

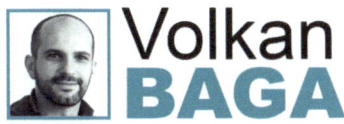

Volkan BAGA

Website: www.volkanbaga.de
Email: mail@volkanbaga.de
Title: Fünf Steine (Five Stones)
Art: Oil on panel 23.6" x 29.5"

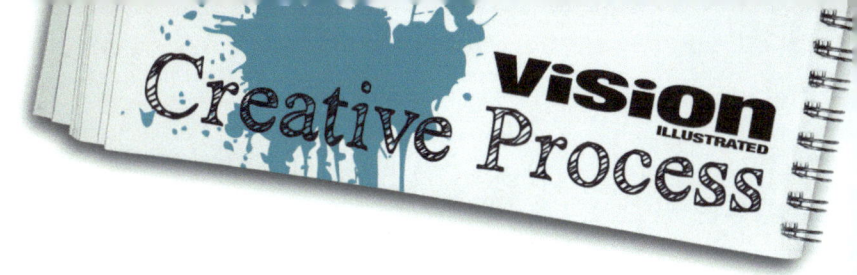

Creative Process

1 Thumbnail Sketches

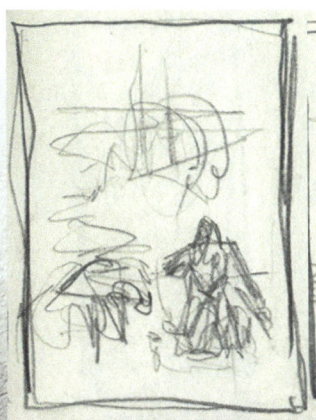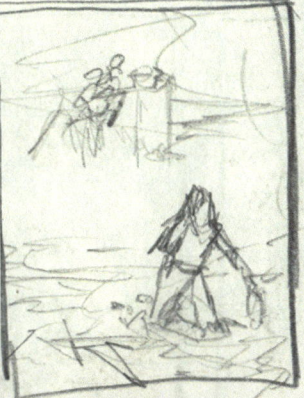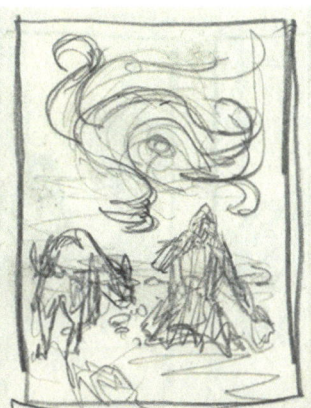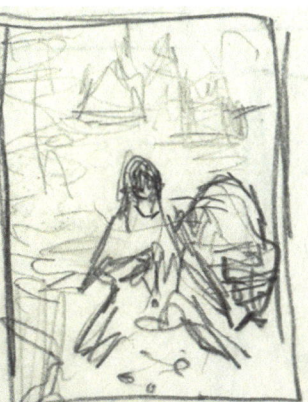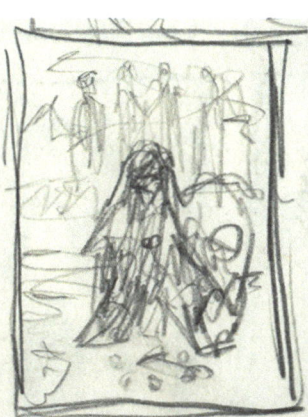

2 Photo Reference

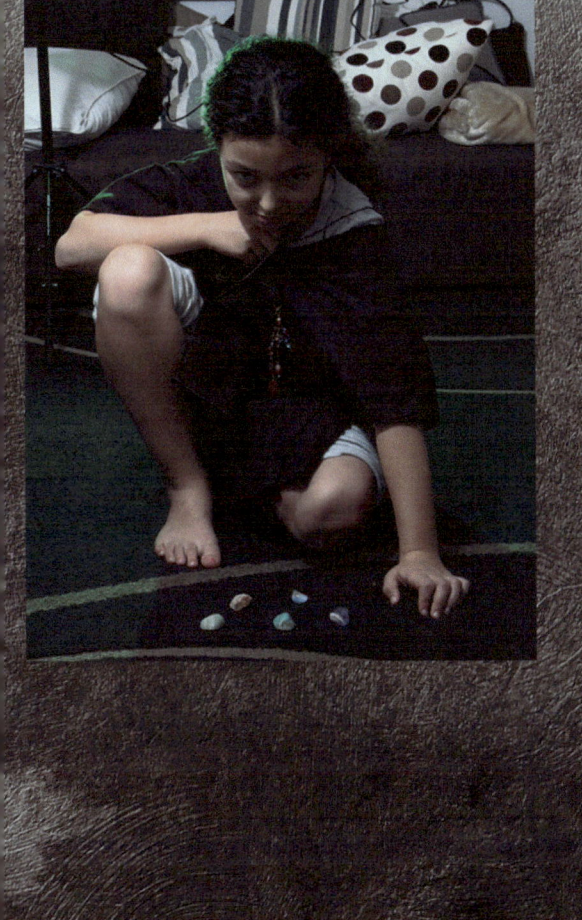

3 Final Drawing

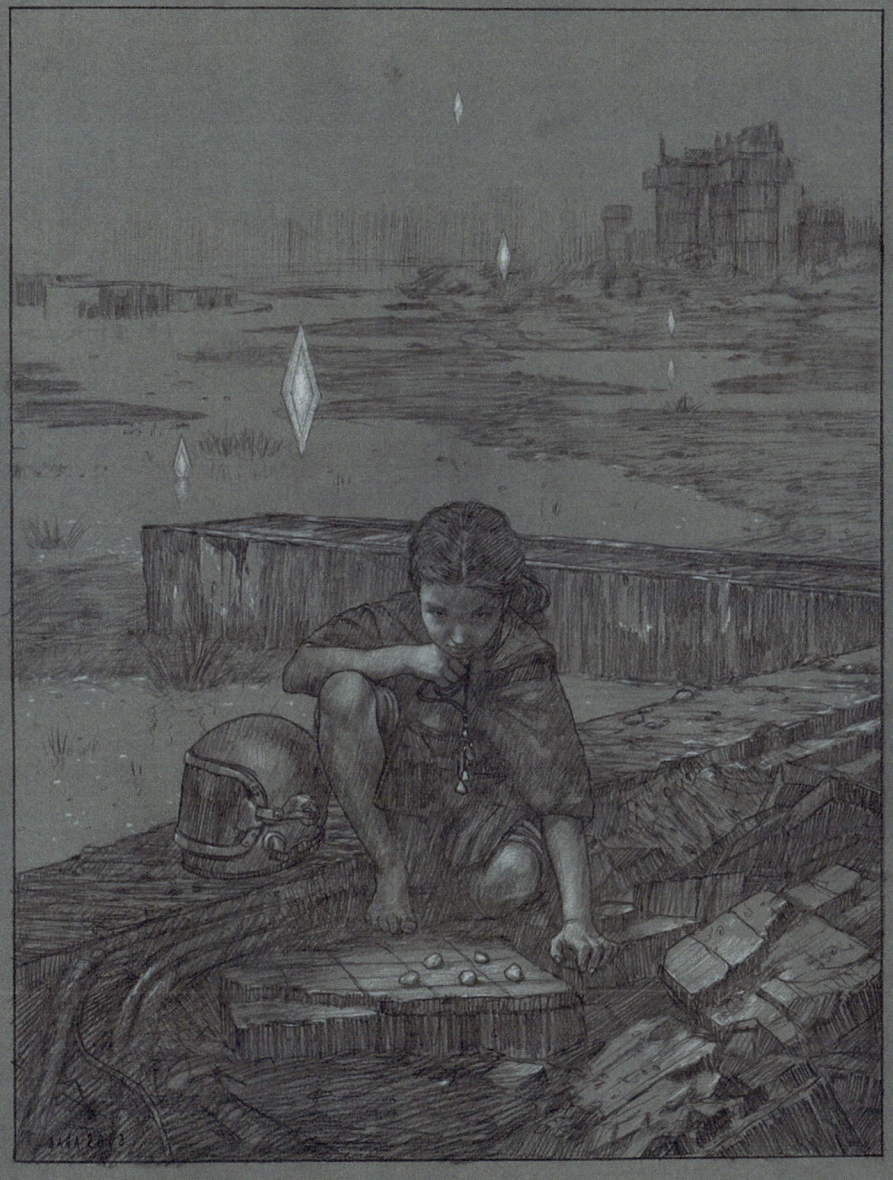

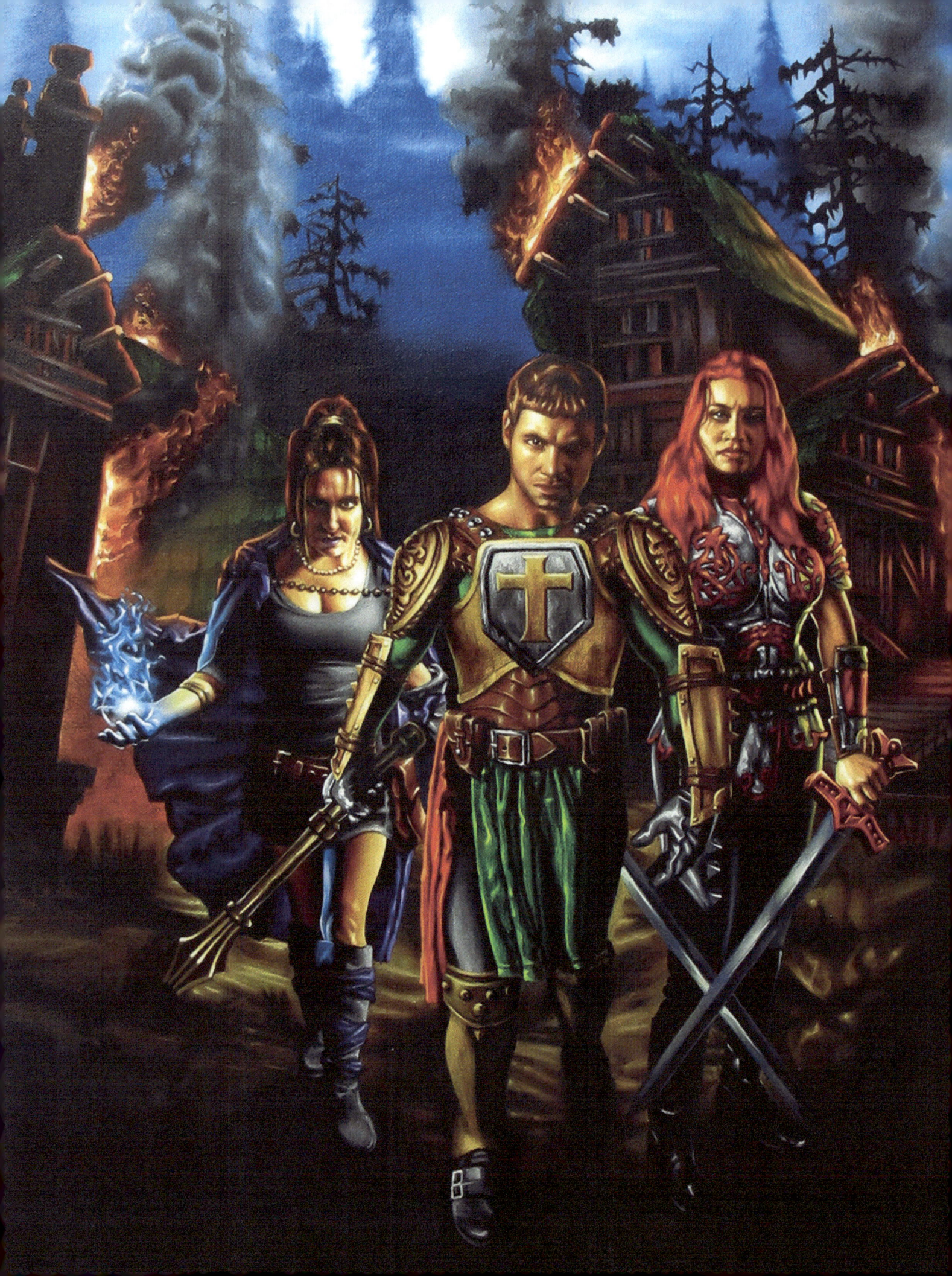

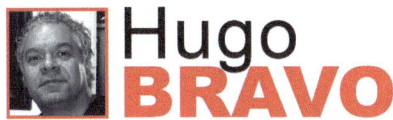

Hugo BRAVO

Website: www.bravoillustrations.com
Email: hugobravo@bravoillustrations.com
Title: Redeem The Knight: Blood Ties
Art: Oil on canvas 18" x 24"

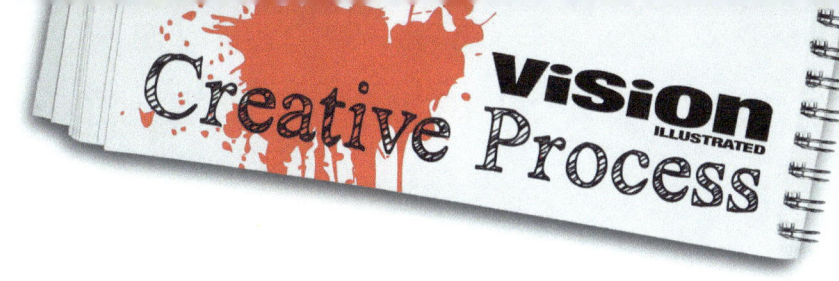

Creative Process

① Character Designs

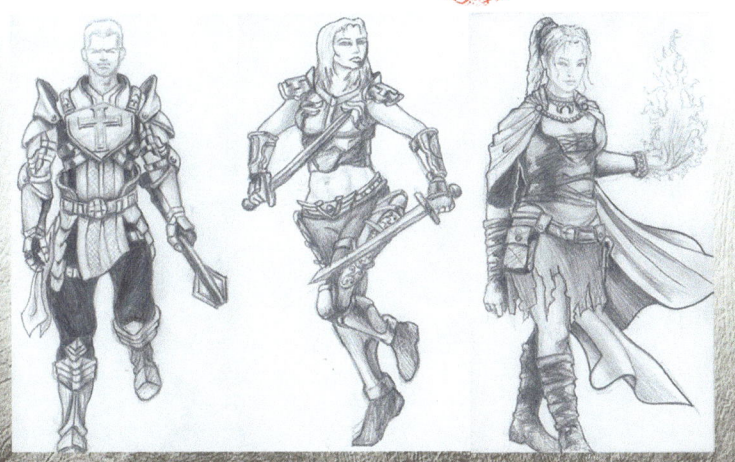

② Photo Reference

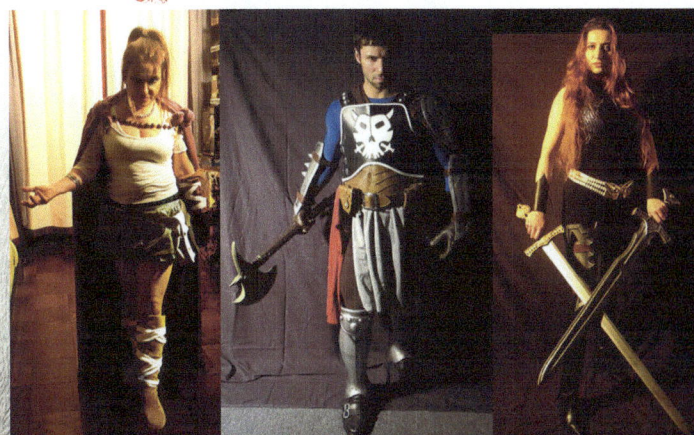

③ Final Drawing

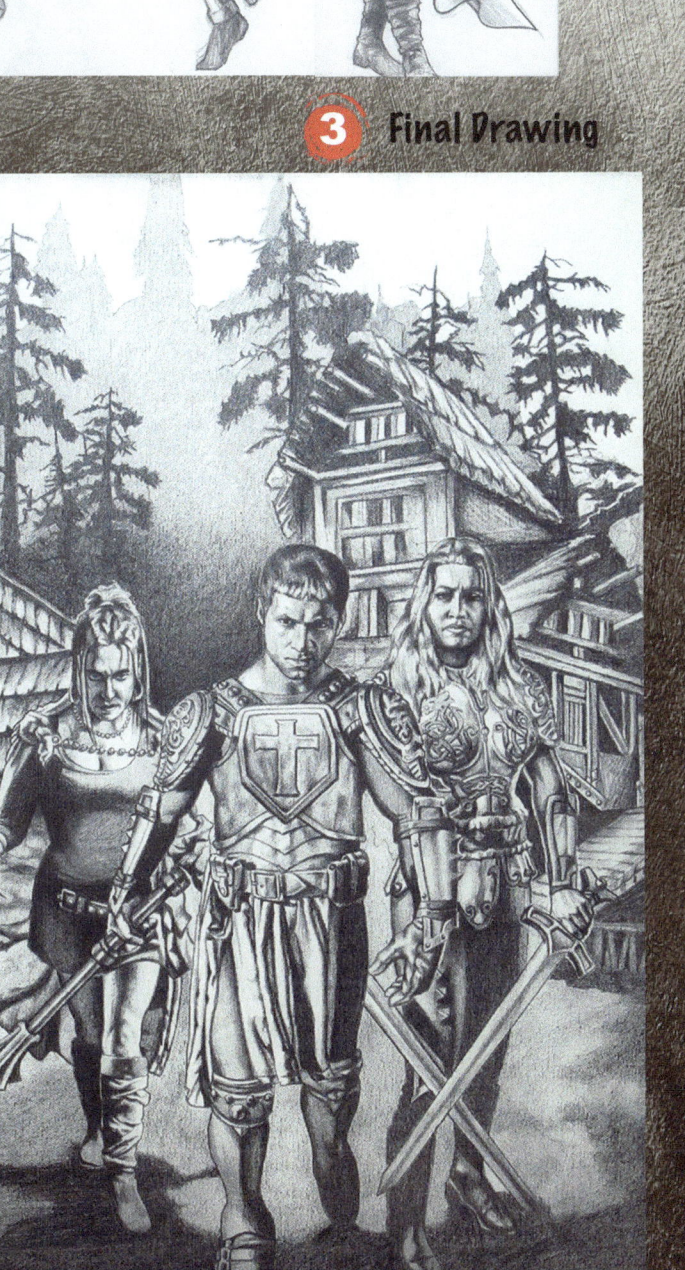

④ Progress Image

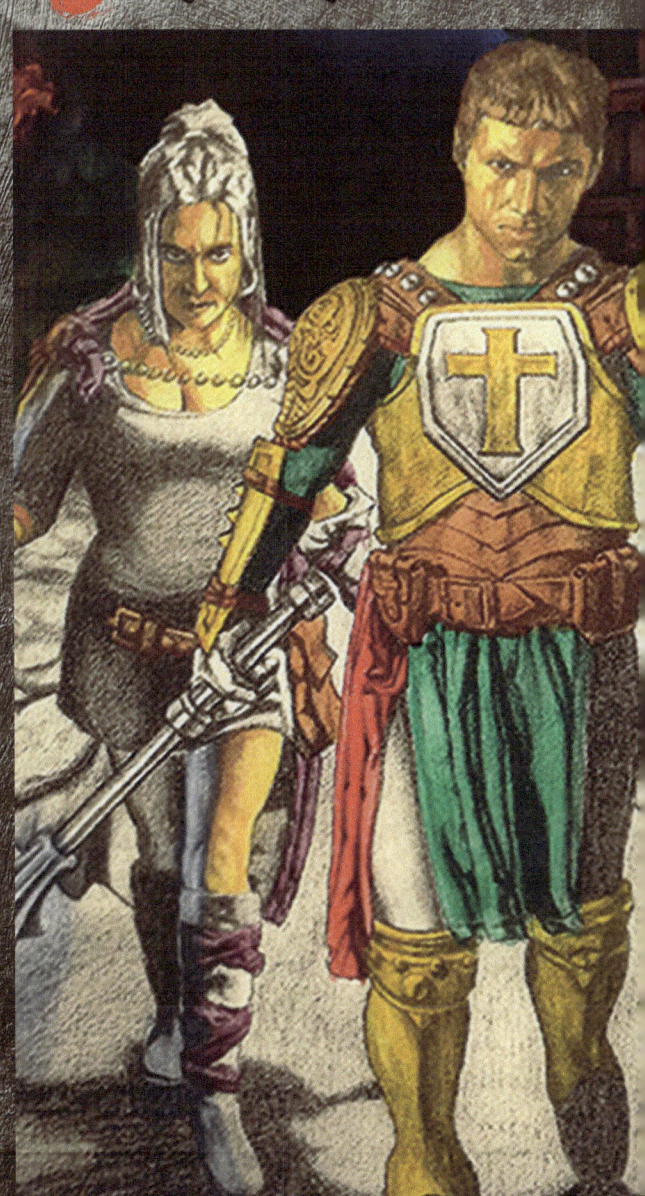

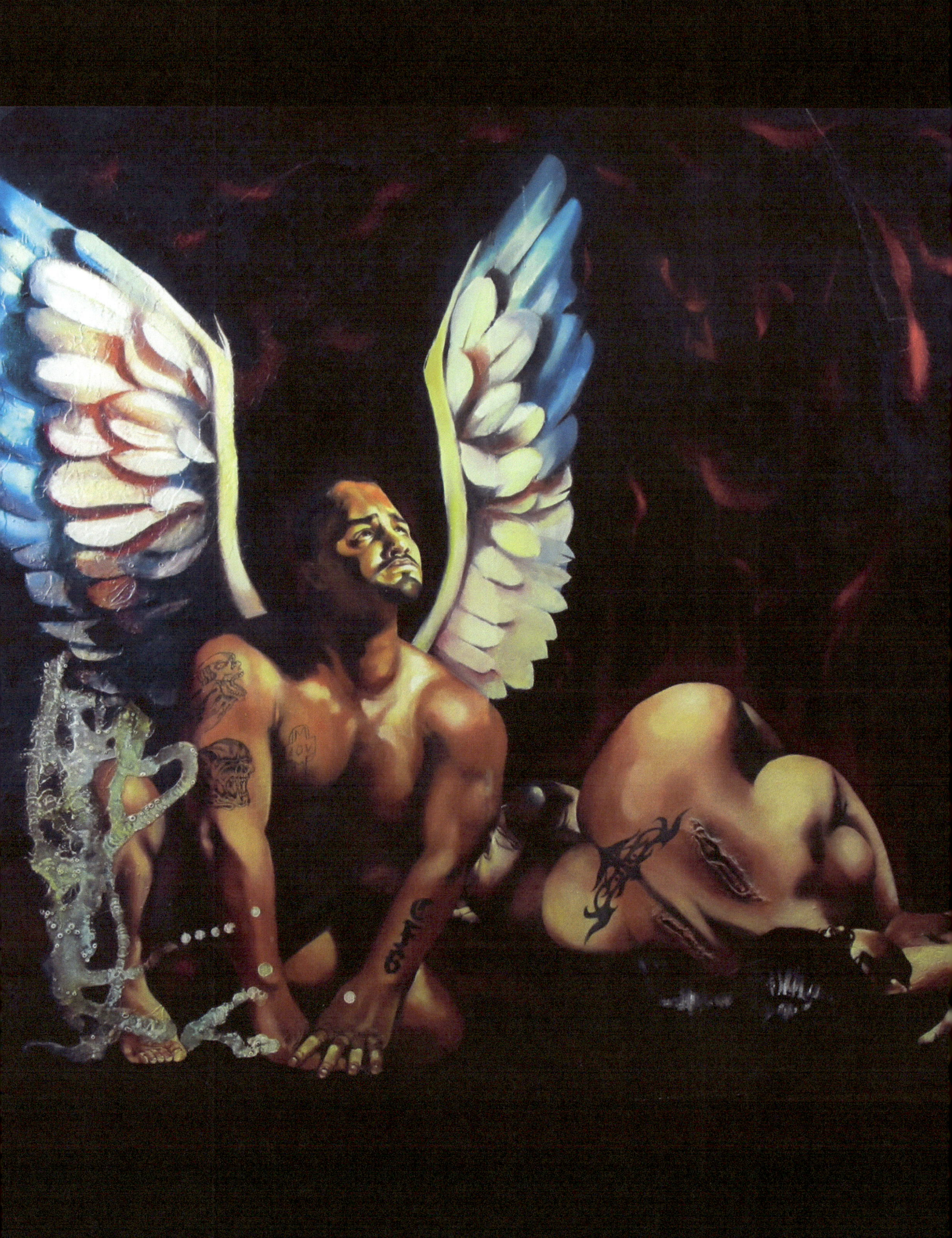

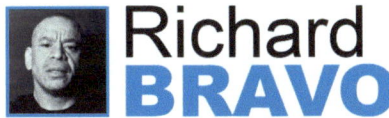

Richard
BRAVO

Website: www.facebook.com/BRAVOARTSNYC1
Email: richardbravo43@gmail.com
Title: Fall From Grace
Art: Oil on Board 48"x48"

Creative Process

① Thumbnail Sketches

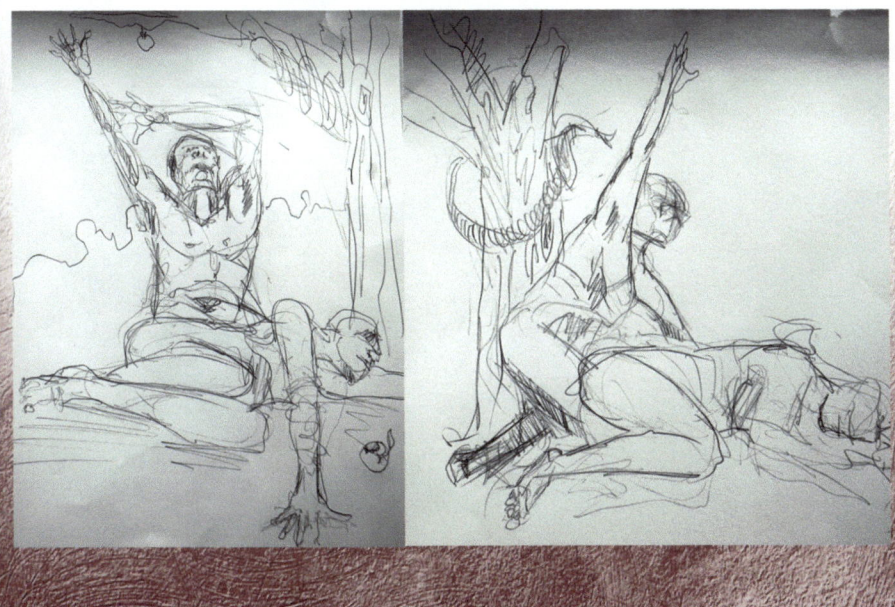

③ Detail Close Ups

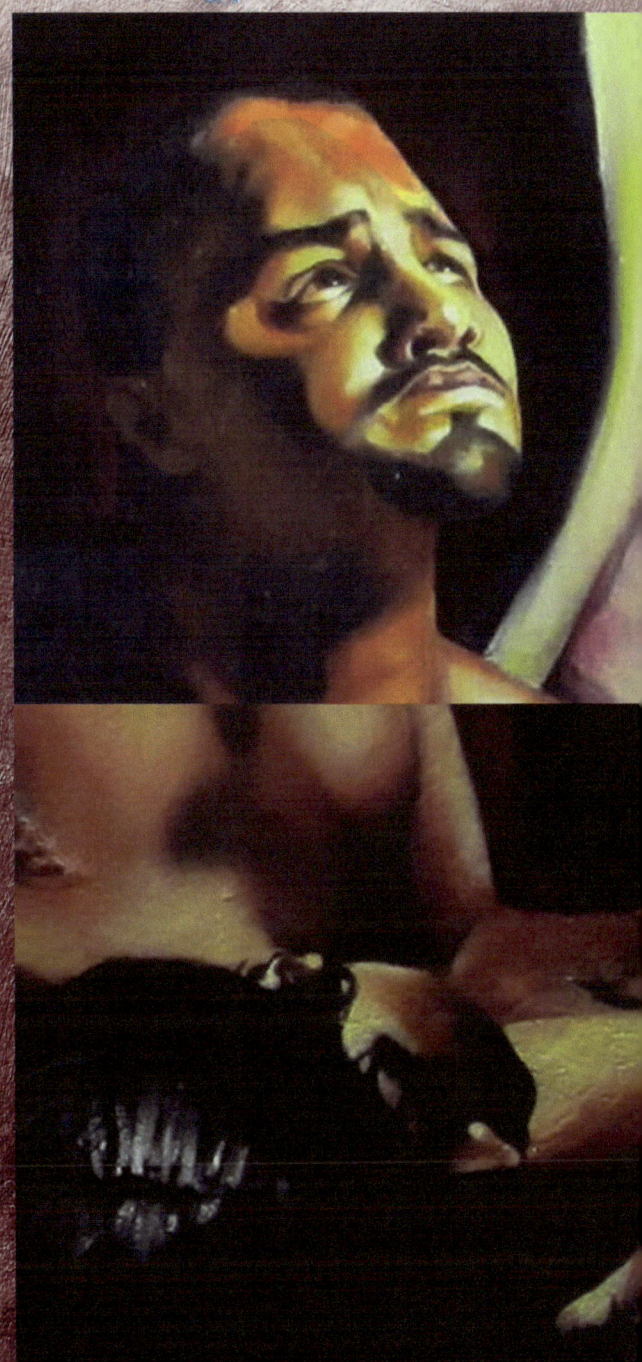

② Final Drawing

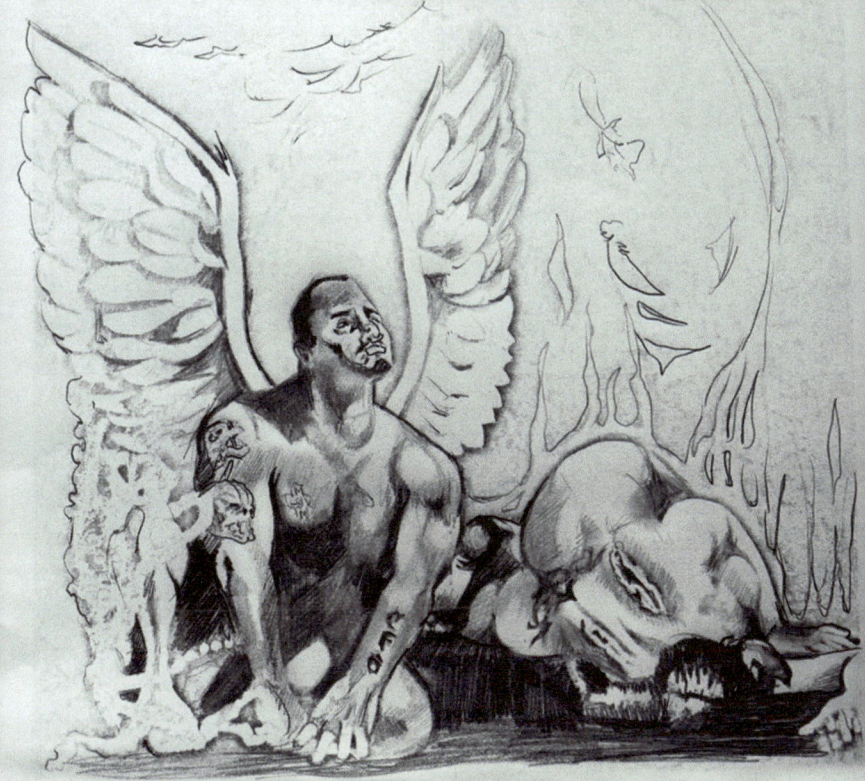

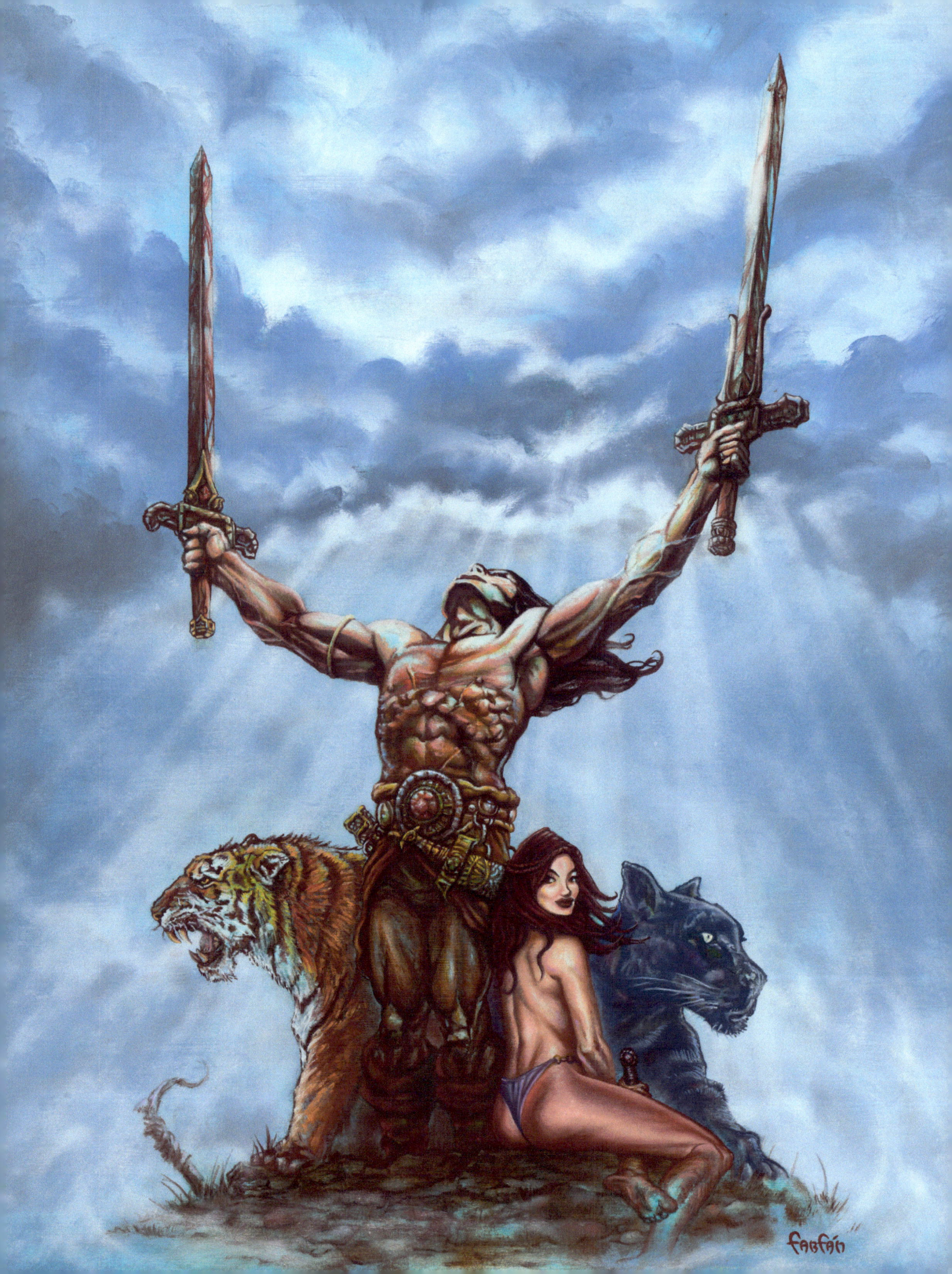

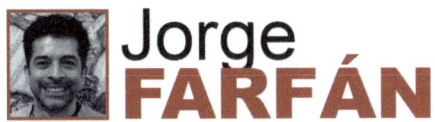

Jorge FARFÁN

Website: www.farfanstudios.com
Email: farfanstudios@yahoo.com
Title: Frazetta Tribute
Art: Oil on coldpress illustration board 15"x20"

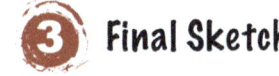

Creative Process — vision ILLUSTRATED

3 Final Sketch

1 Thumbnail Sketches

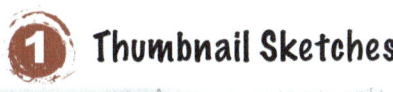

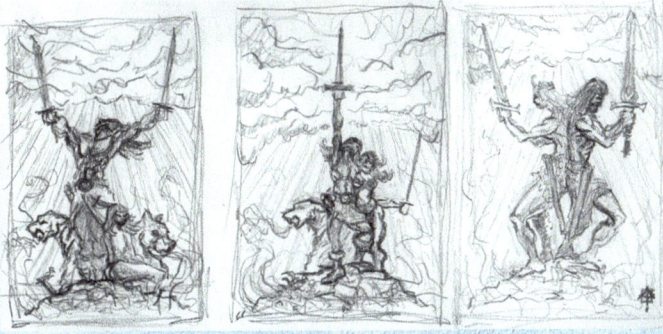

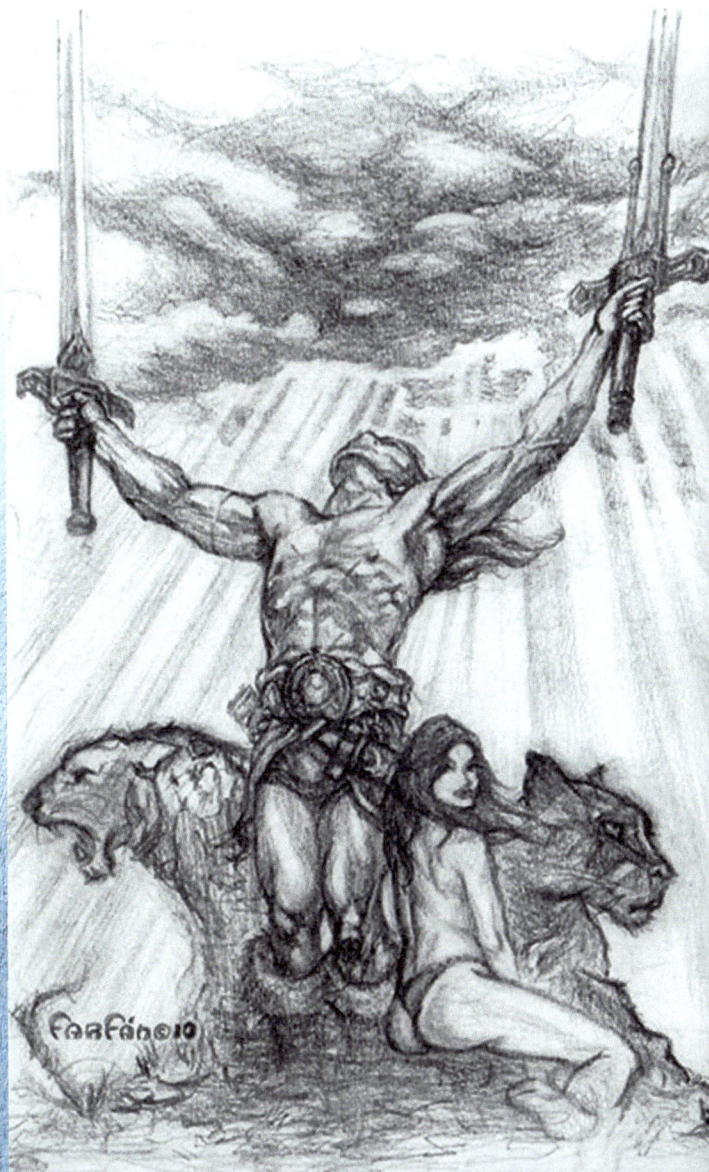

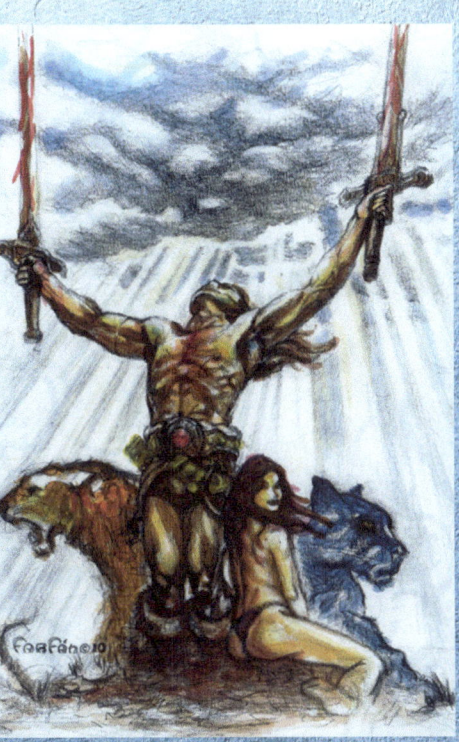

2 Color Study

4 Progress Images

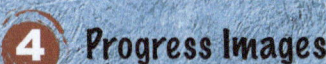

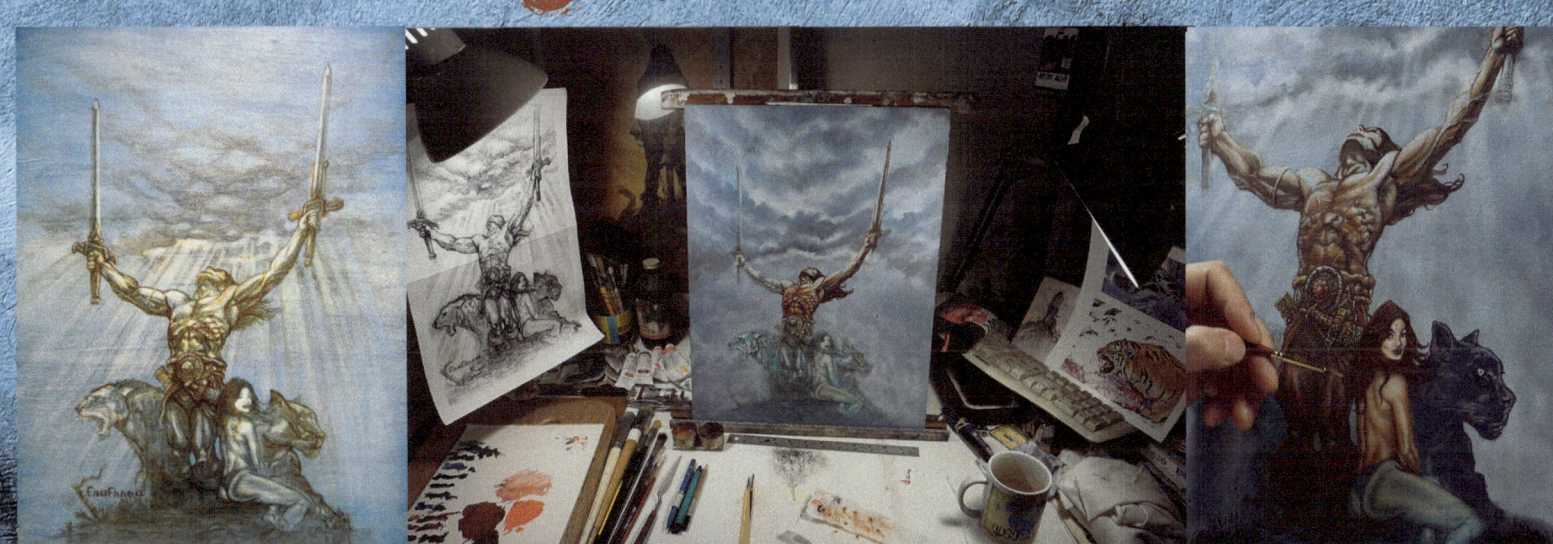

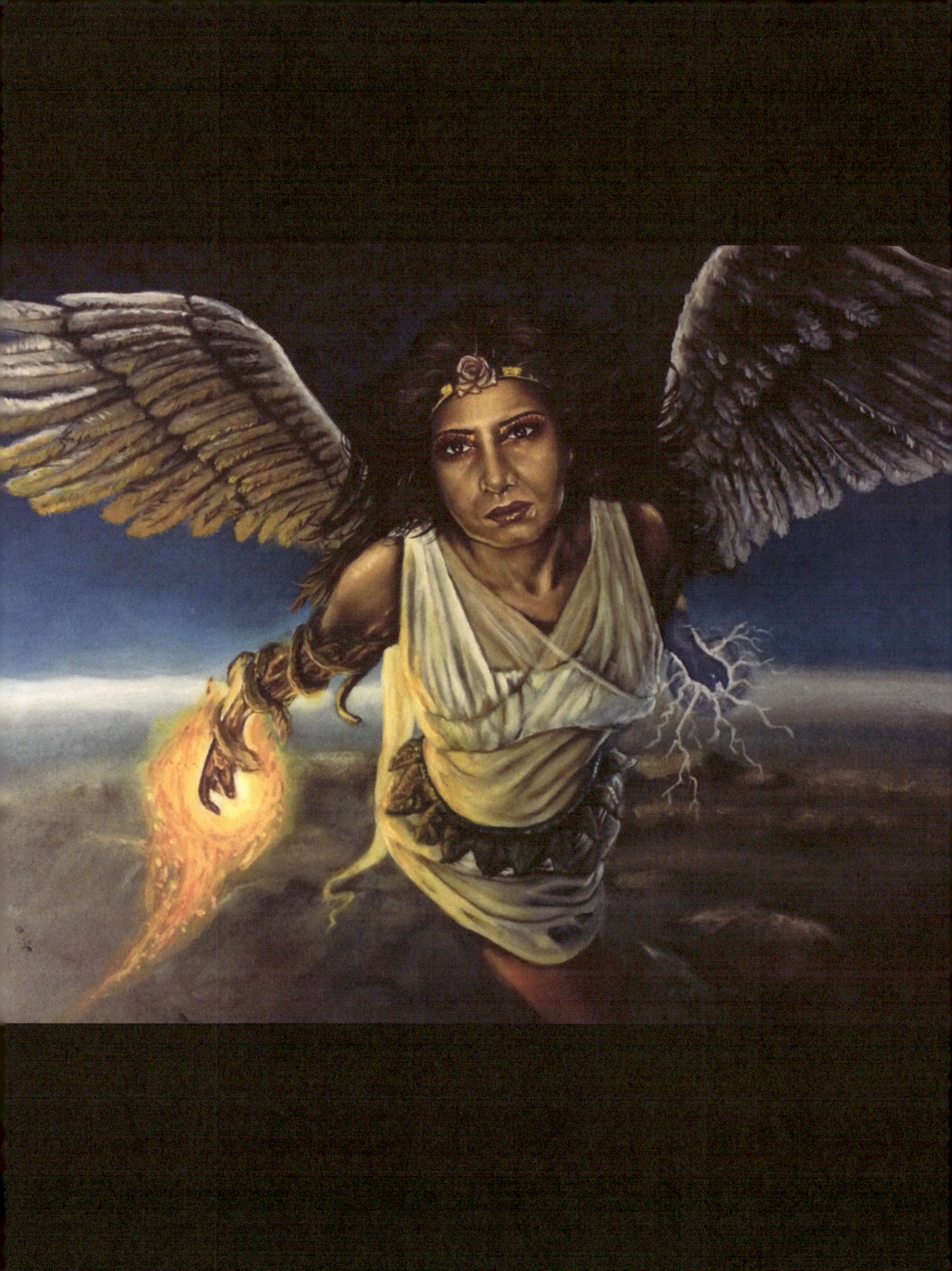

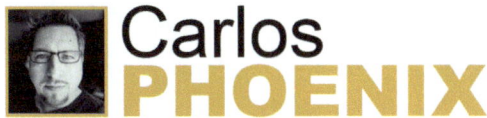

Carlos PHOENIX

Website: www.carlosphoenix.com
Email: carlosphoenix@gmail.com
Title: War Angel
Art: Oil on masonite 24" x 36"

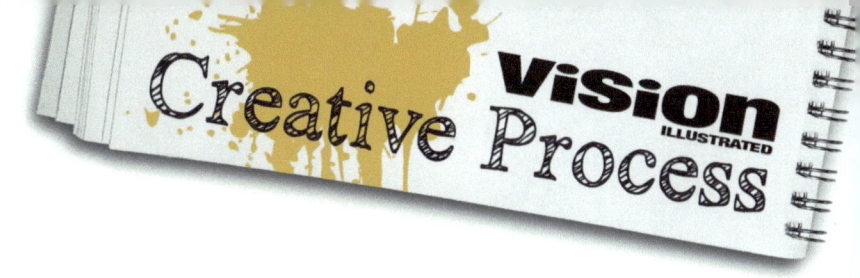
 4 **Progress Images**

1

Thumbnail Sketch

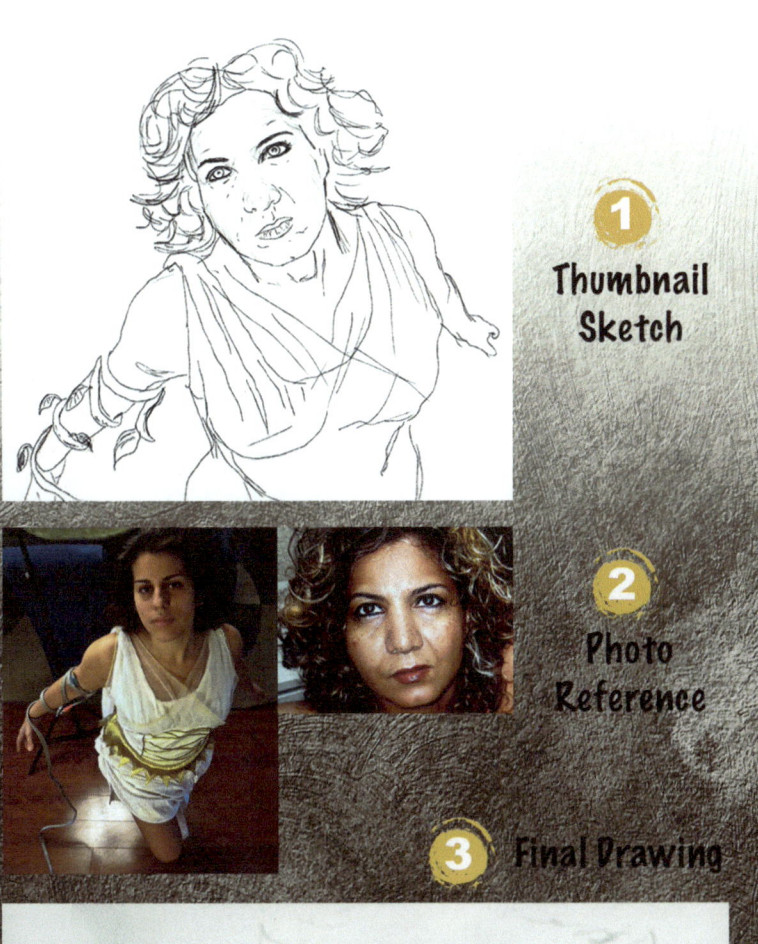

2

Photo Reference

3 **Final Drawing**

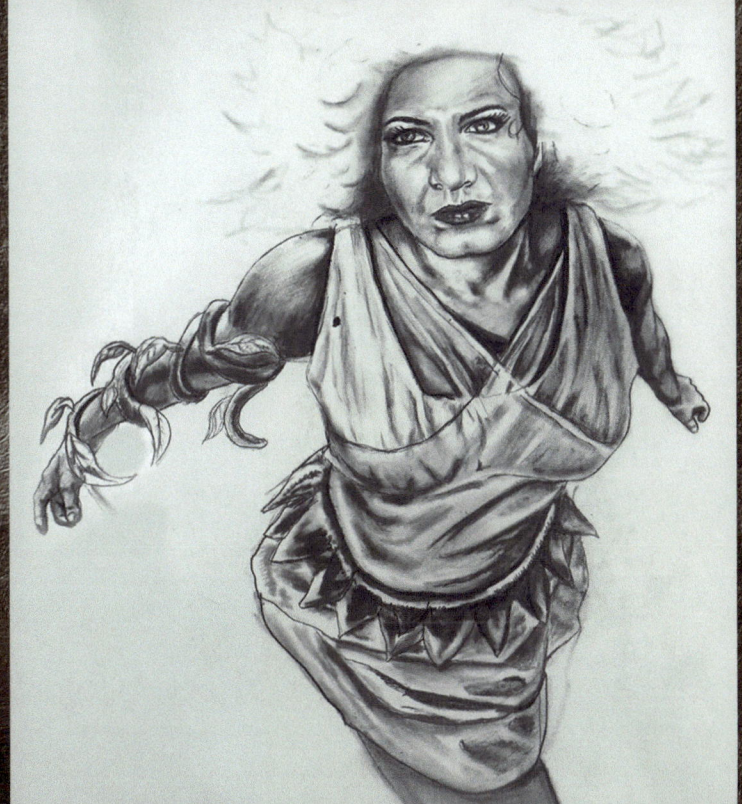

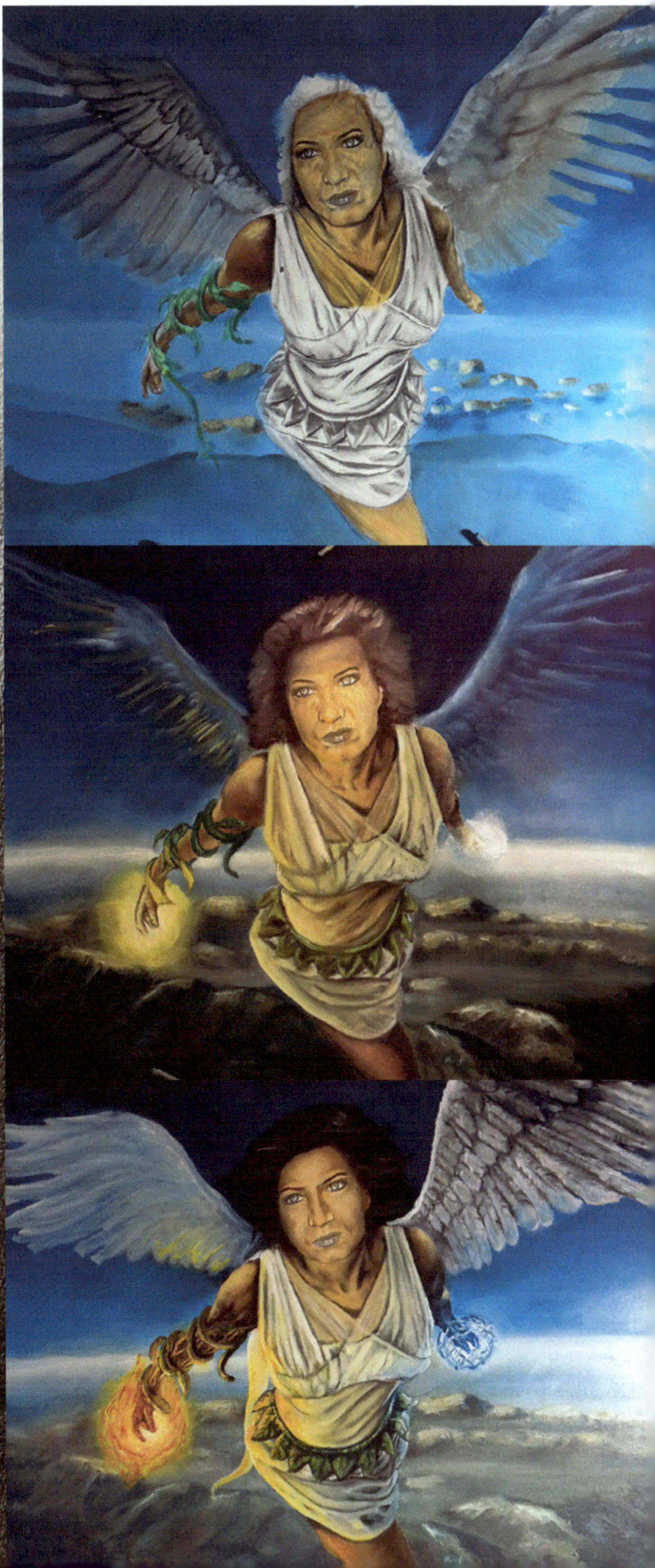

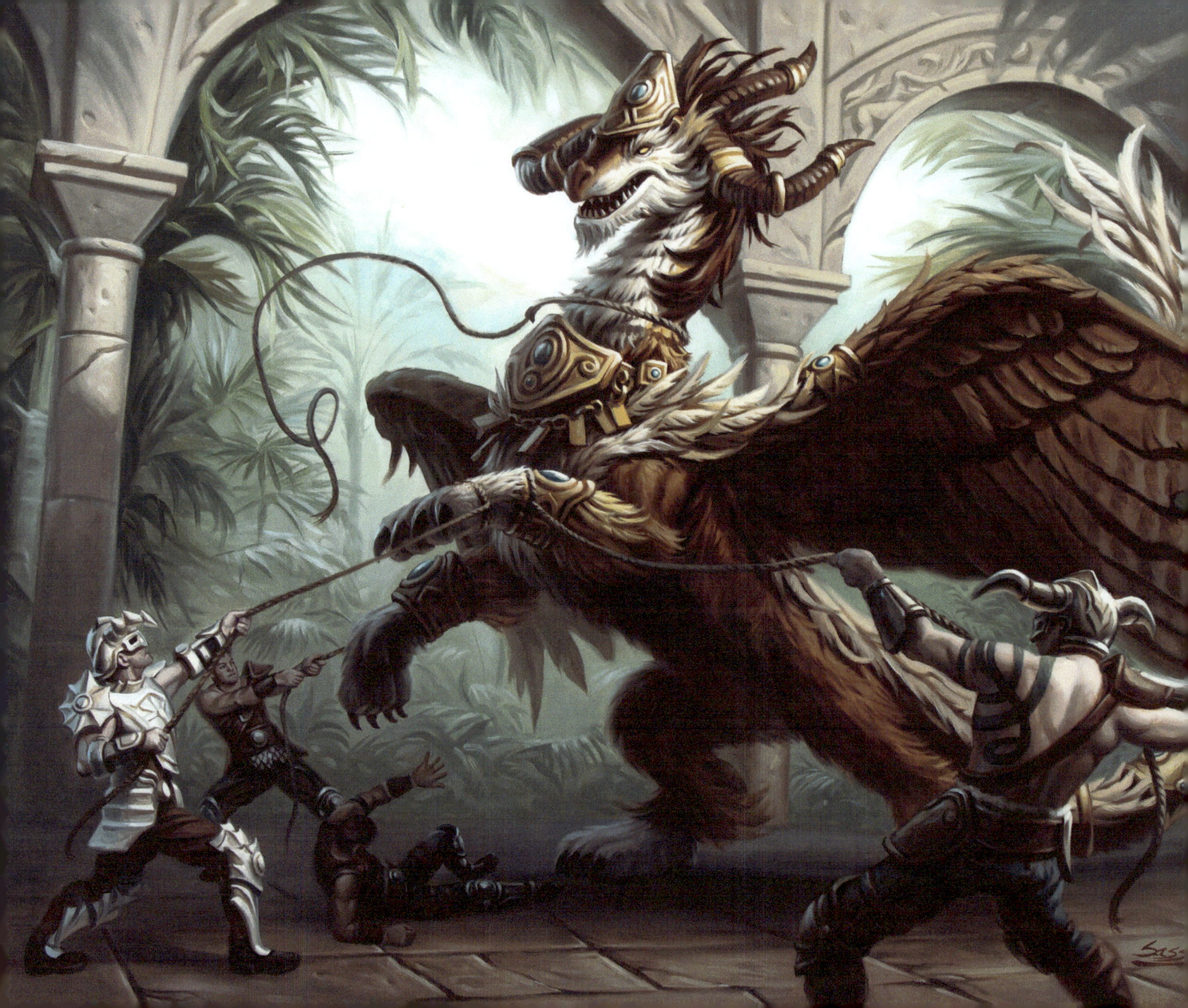

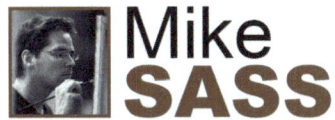

Mike SASS

Website: www.sassart.com
Title: Zios the Cloudburster
Art: Oil on panel 14" x 18"

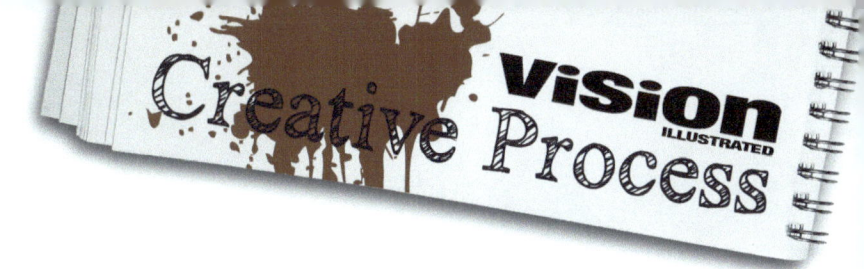

Creative Vision Process
ILLUSTRATED

1 Thumbnail Sketches

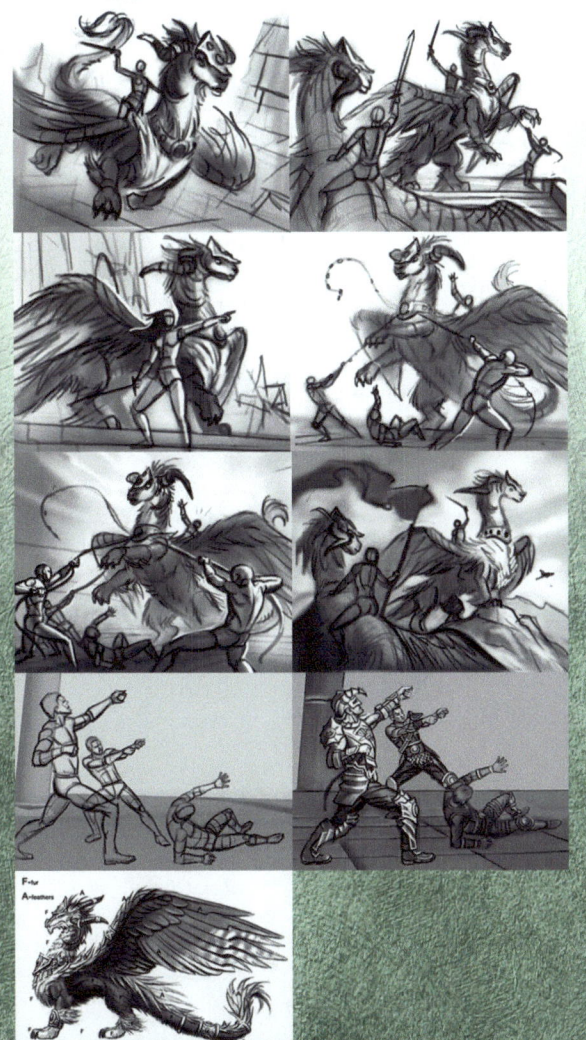

2 Photo Reference

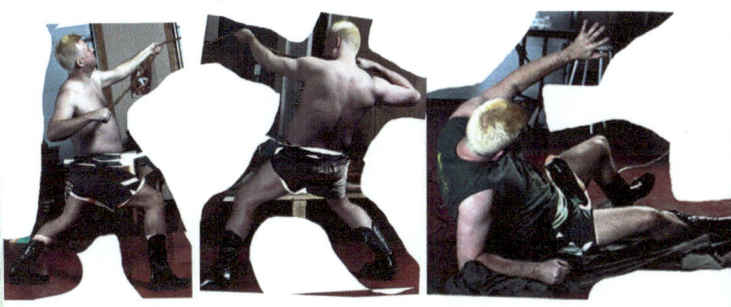

3 Color Study

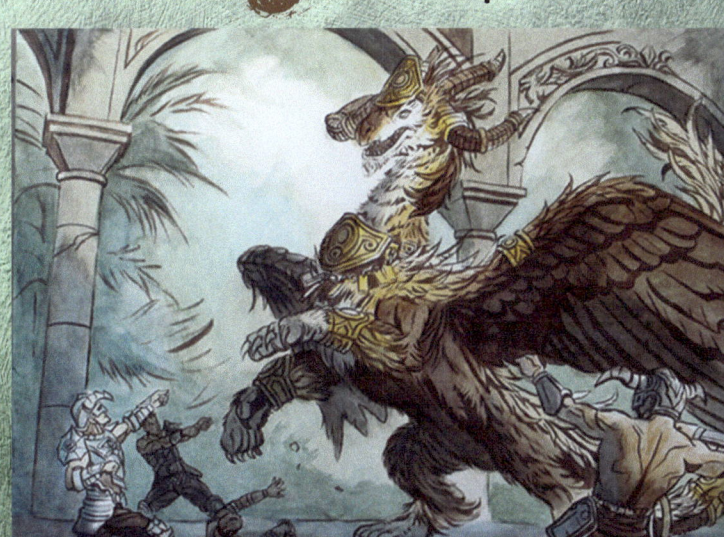

4 Underpainting

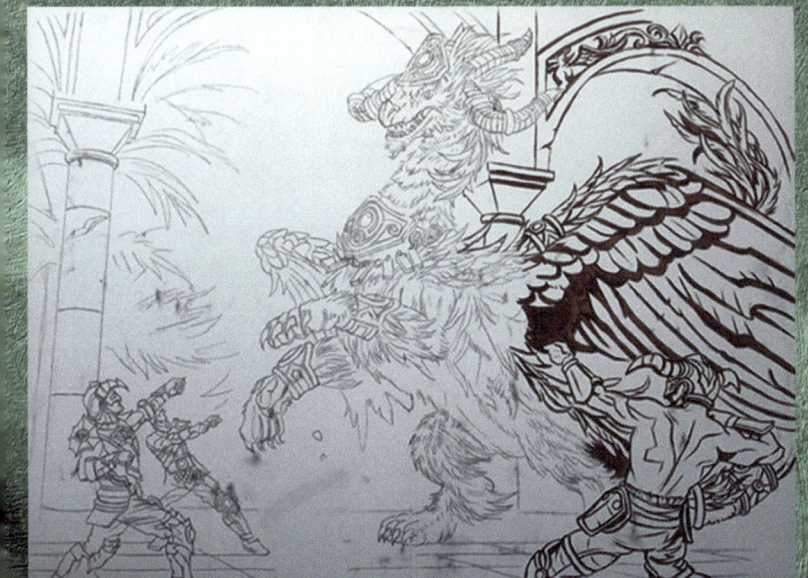

5 Progress Image

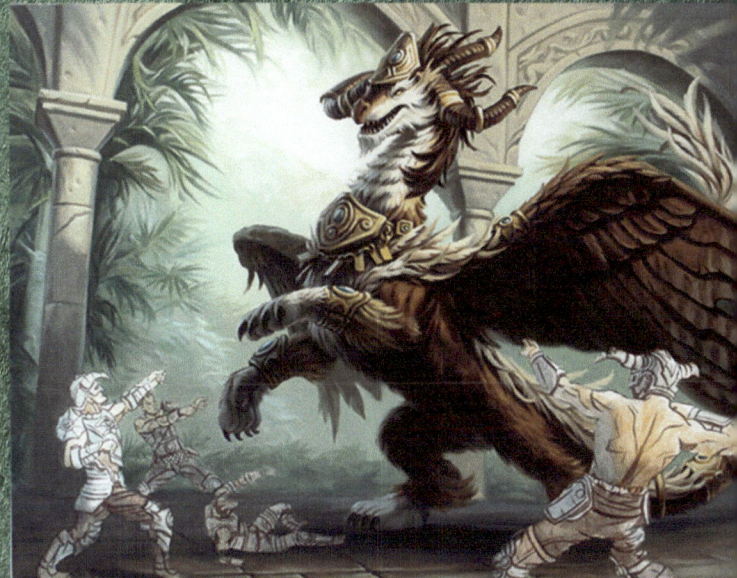

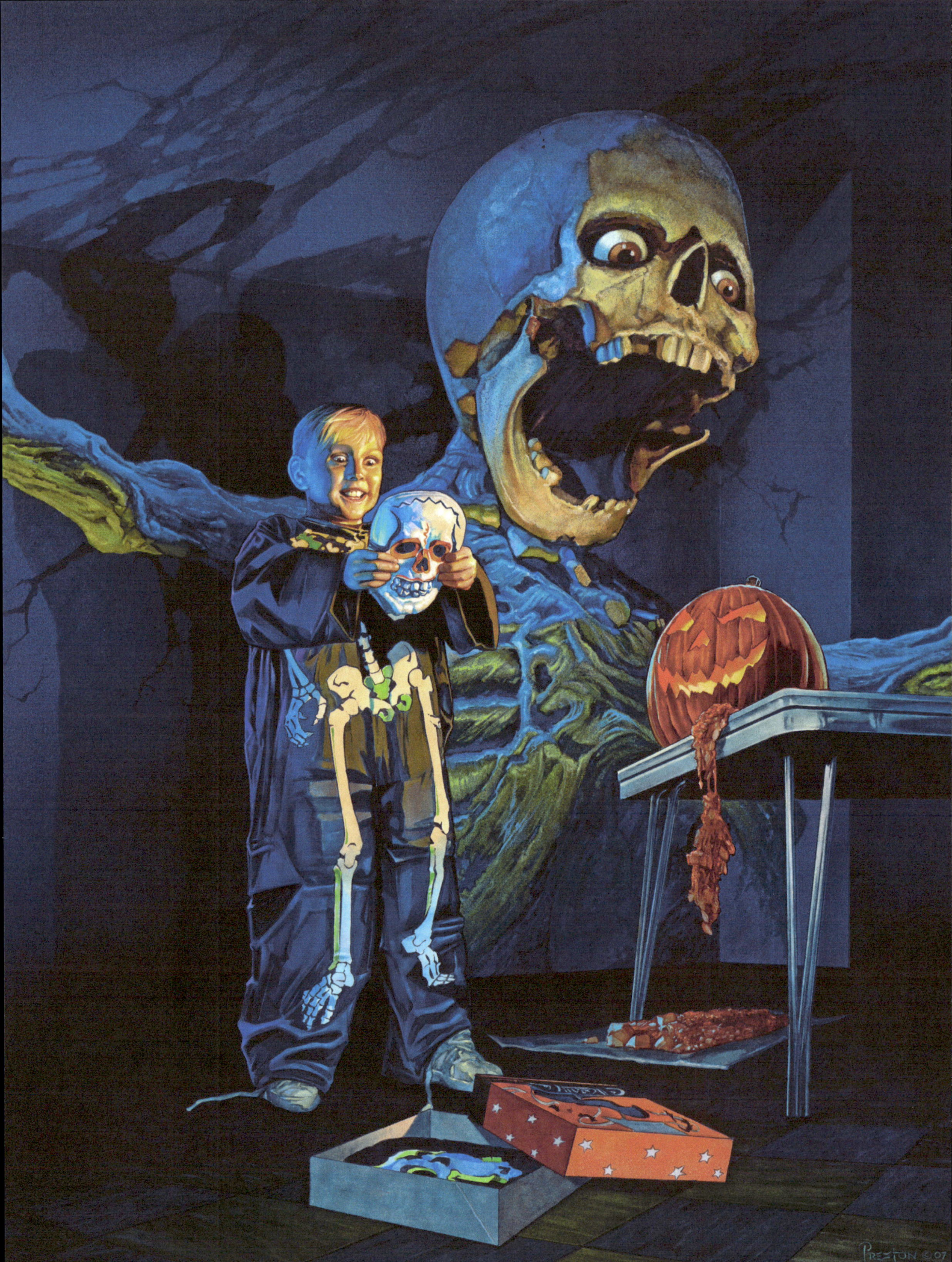

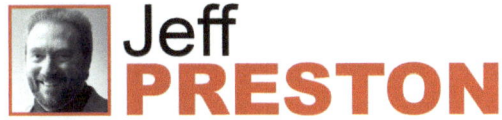

Jeff PRESTON

Website: www.jeffpreston.net
Email: info@jeffpreston.net
Title: The Costume
Art: Prismacolor Markers, Zig Twin Markers, Color Pencil 18" x 22"

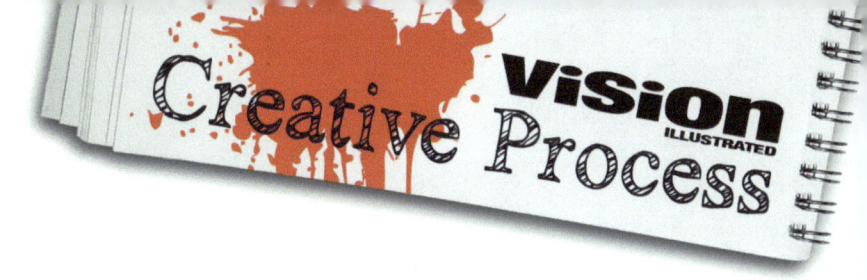

Creative Process

1 Thumbnail Sketches

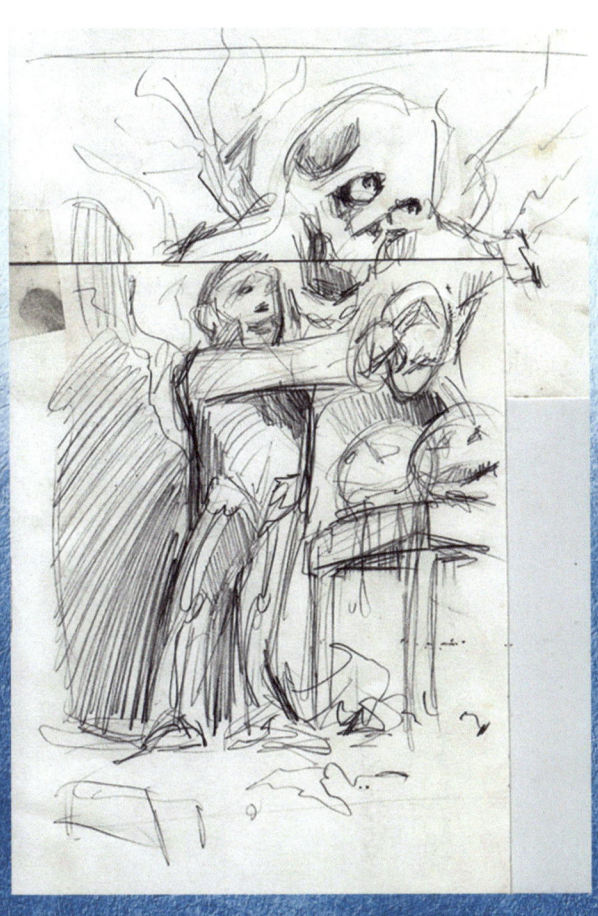

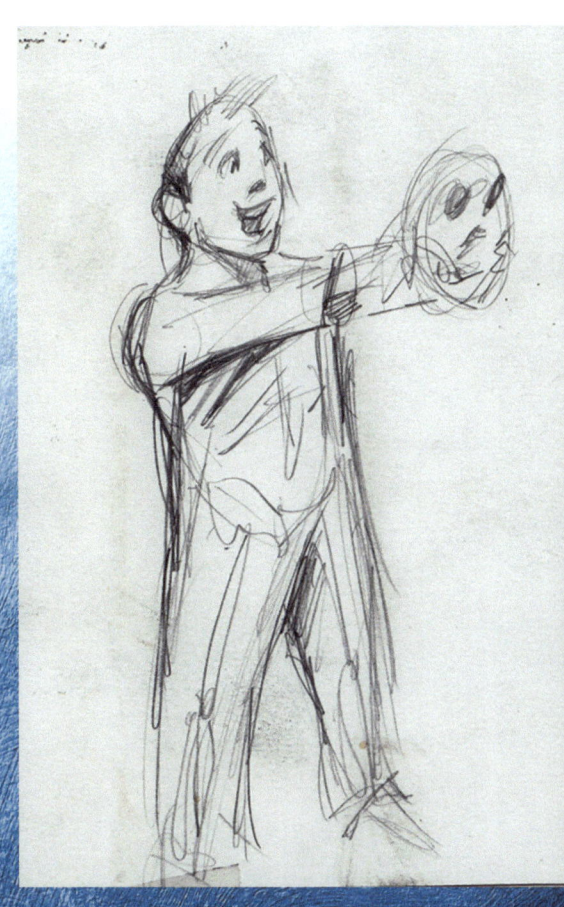

2 Photo Reference

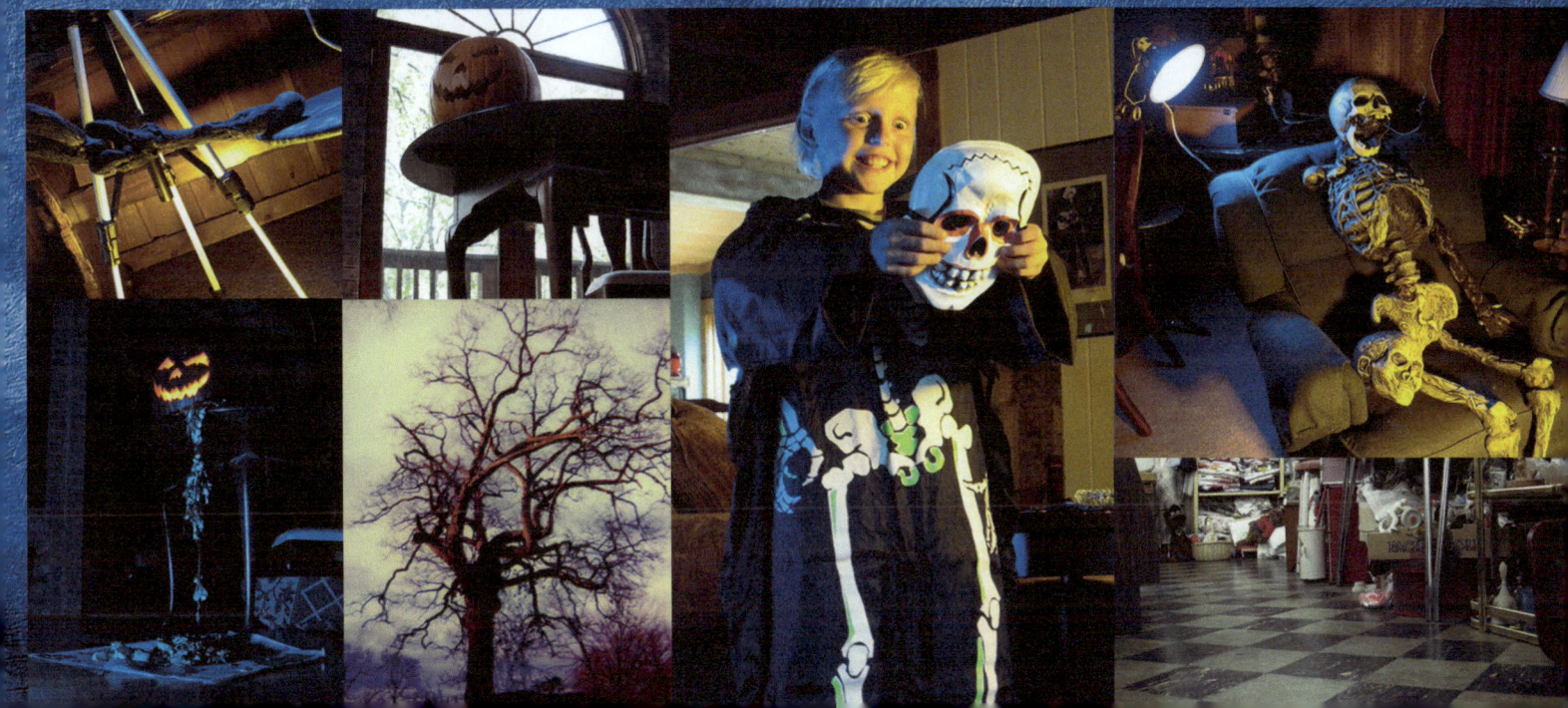

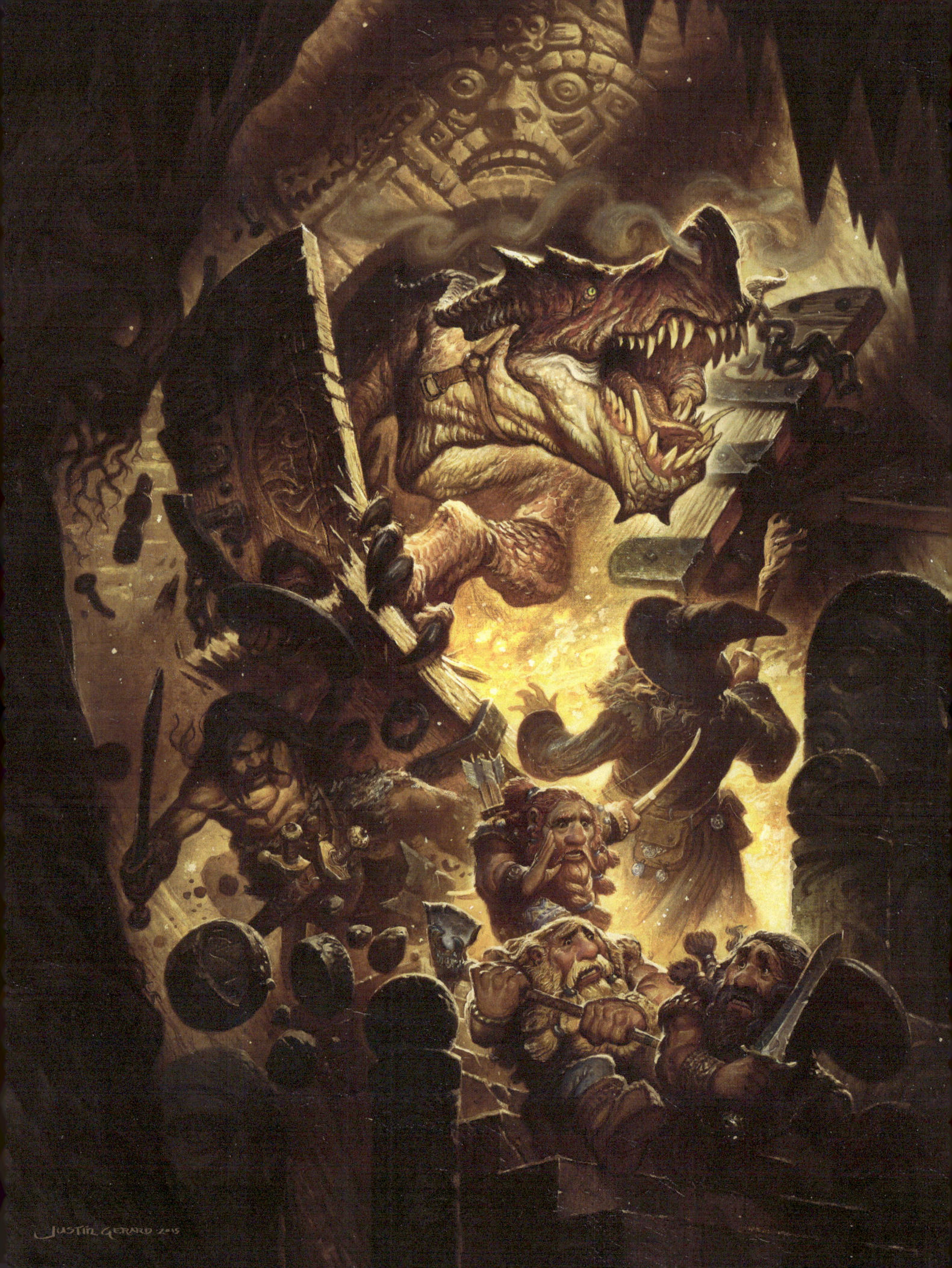

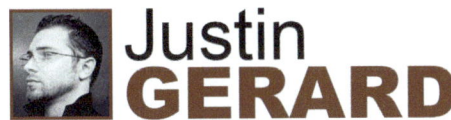

Justin GERARD

Website: www.gallerygerard.com
Email: justingerardillustration@gmail.com
Title: The Wrong Door
Art: Water Color, Ink, Digital 12" x 18"

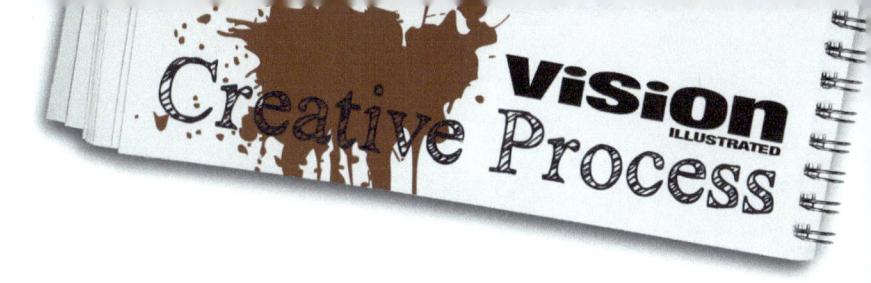
Creative Vision Process

1 Thumbnail Sketches

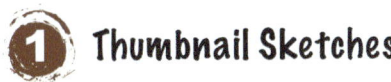
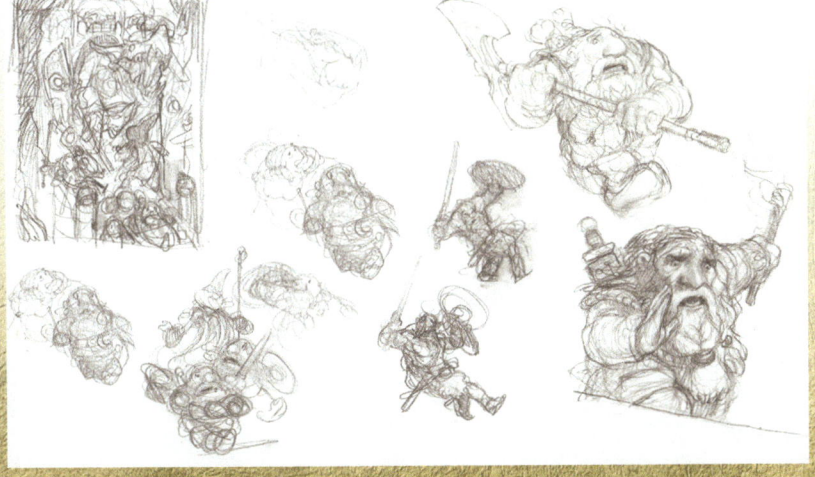

2 Black and White Study

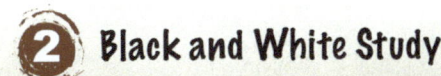

3 Final Drawing

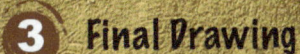
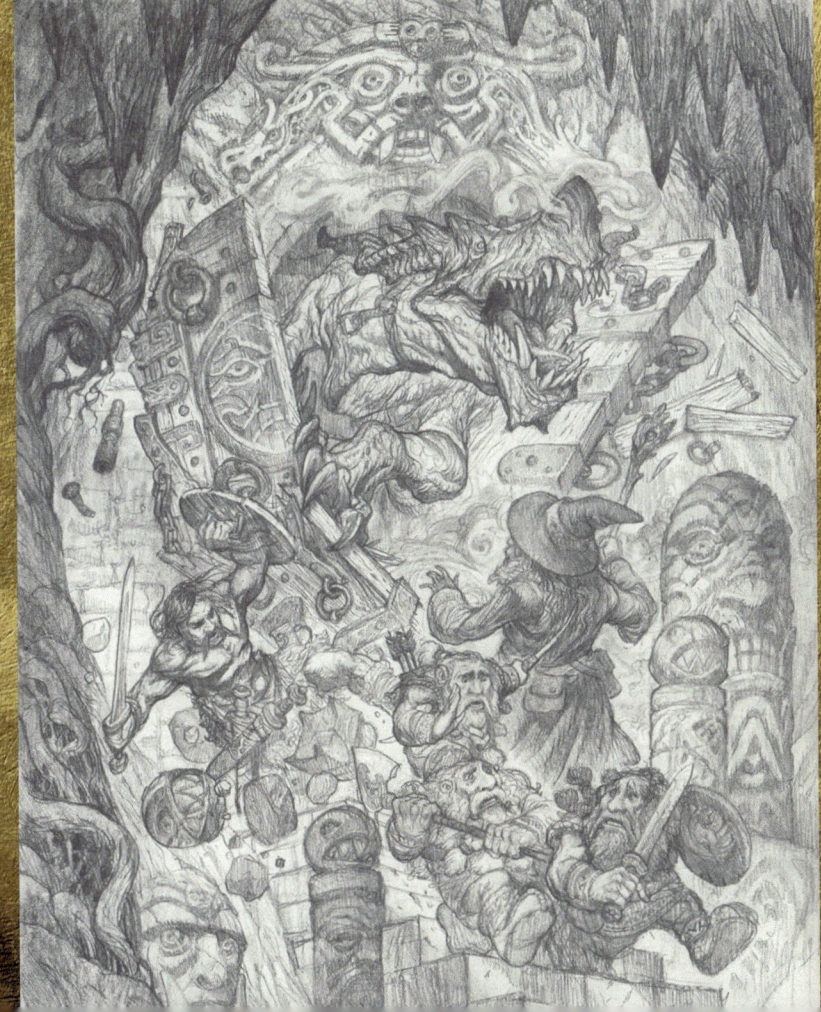

4 Progress Image

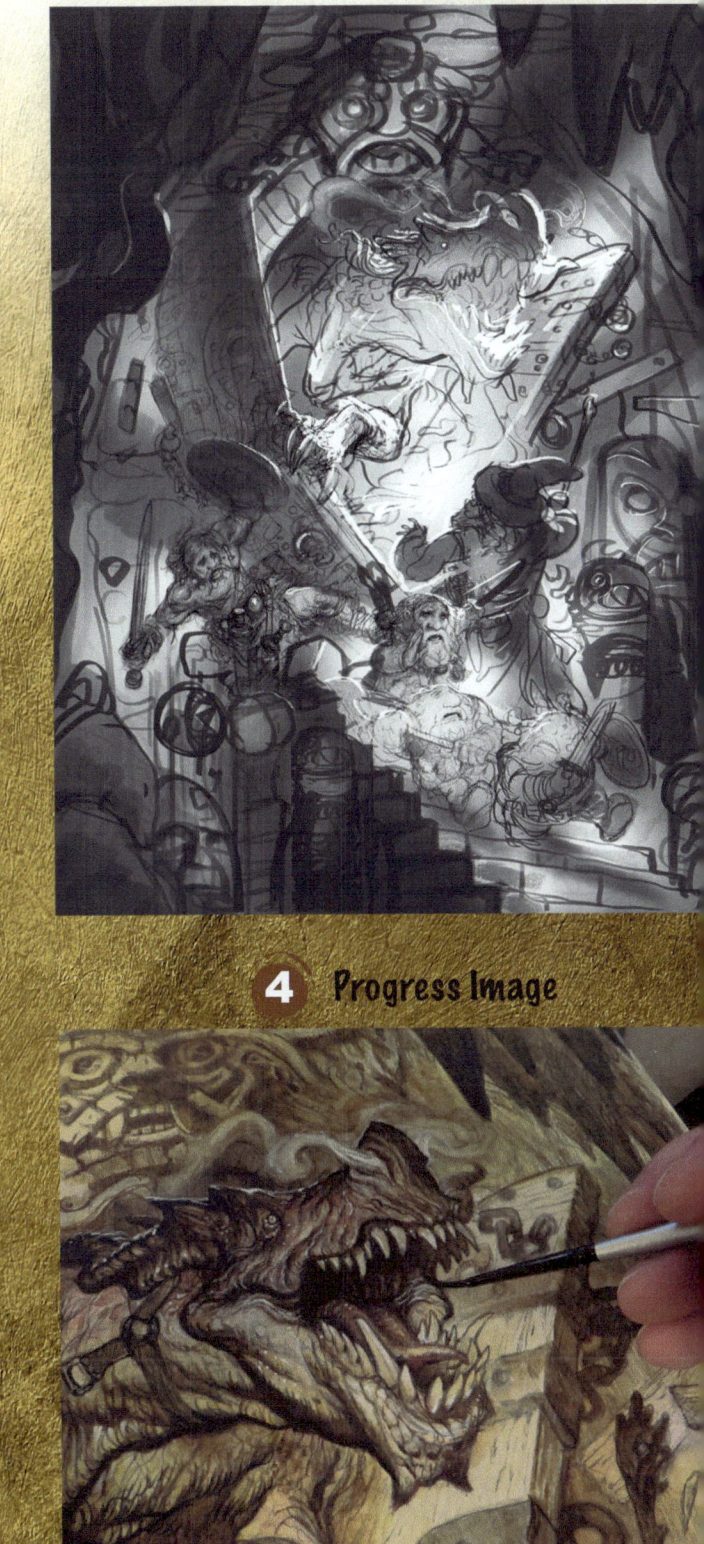

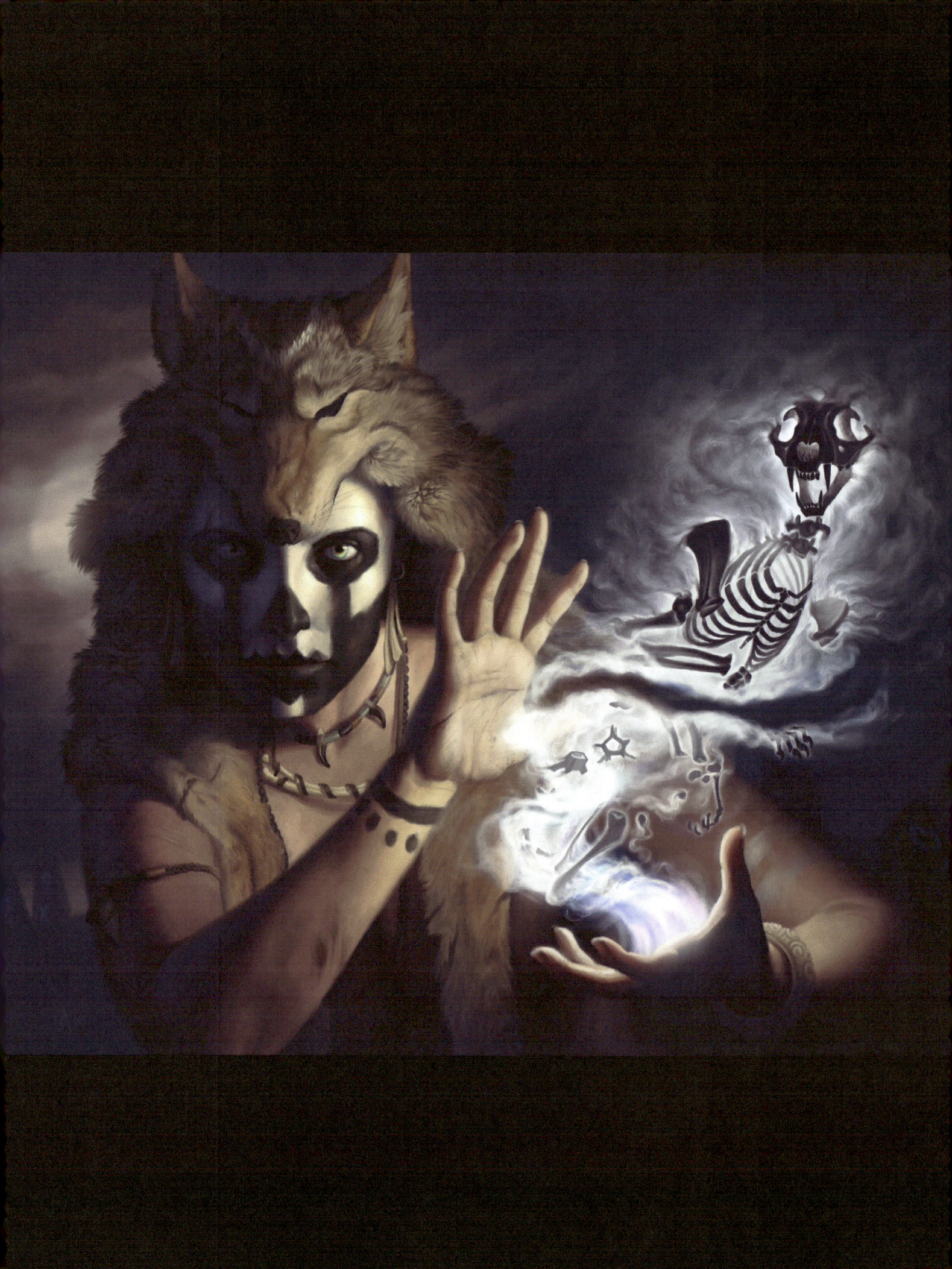

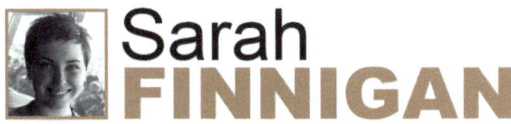

Sarah FINNIGAN

Website: www.sarahfinnigan-art.com
Email: sarahfinnigan.art@gmail.com
Title: Apprentice Bone Summoner
Art: Digital 26.75" x 19.75"

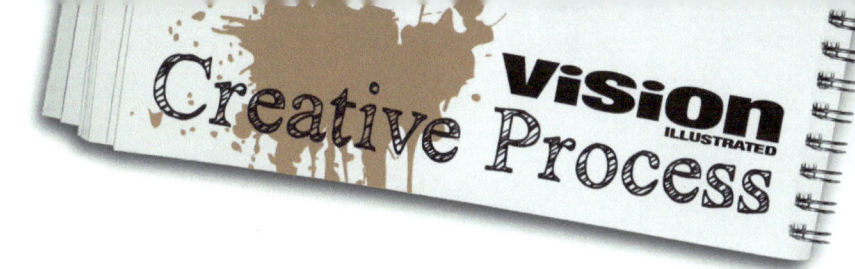

Creative Process — **VISION** ILLUSTRATED

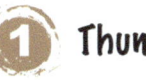 **1** Thumbnail Sketches

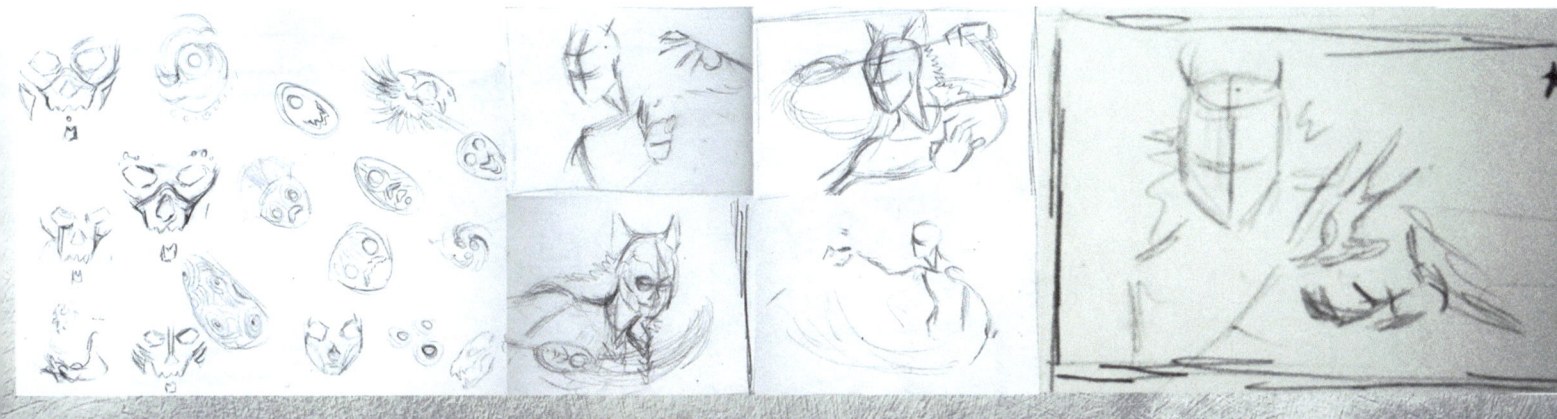

2 Color Study

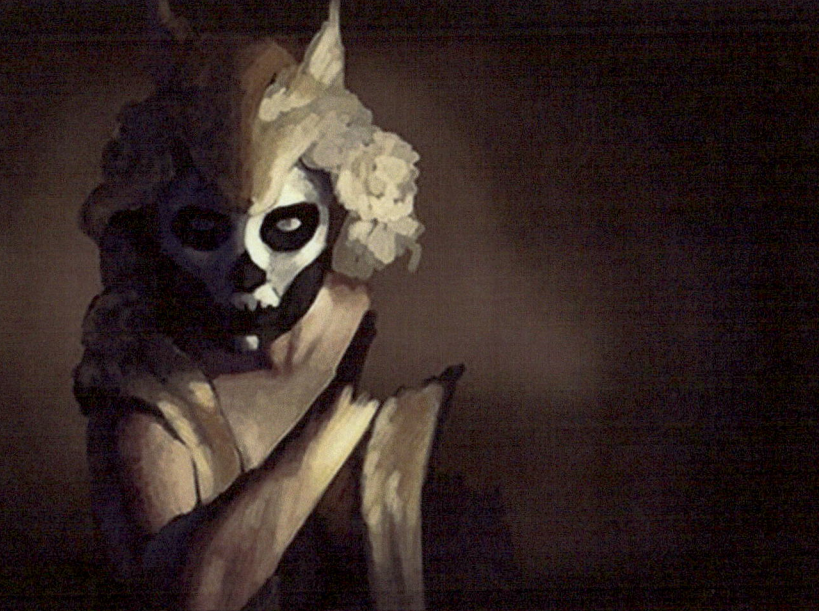

3 Progress Images

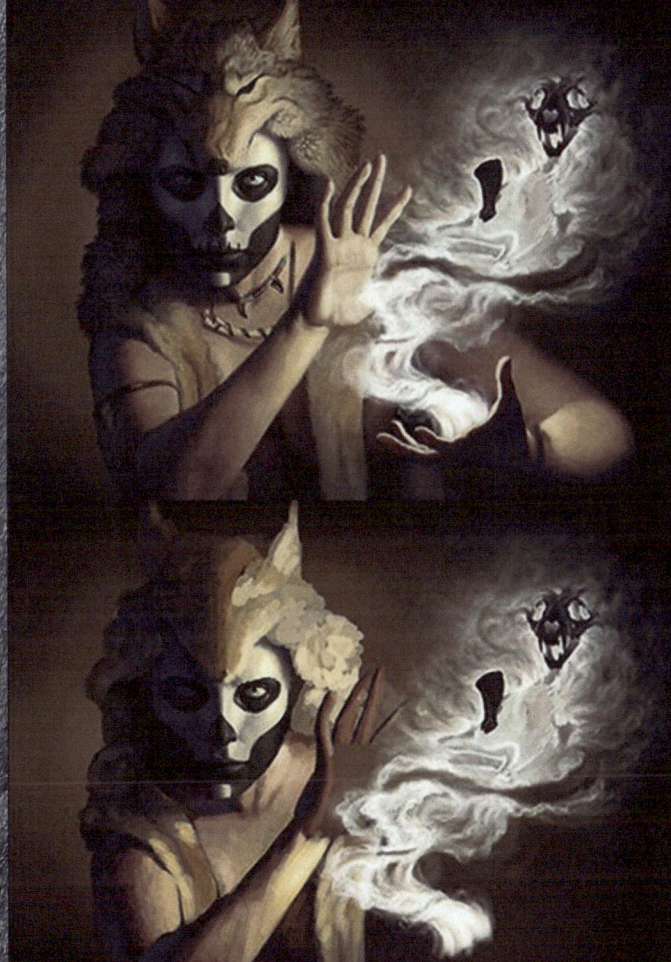

4 Adjustment Notes

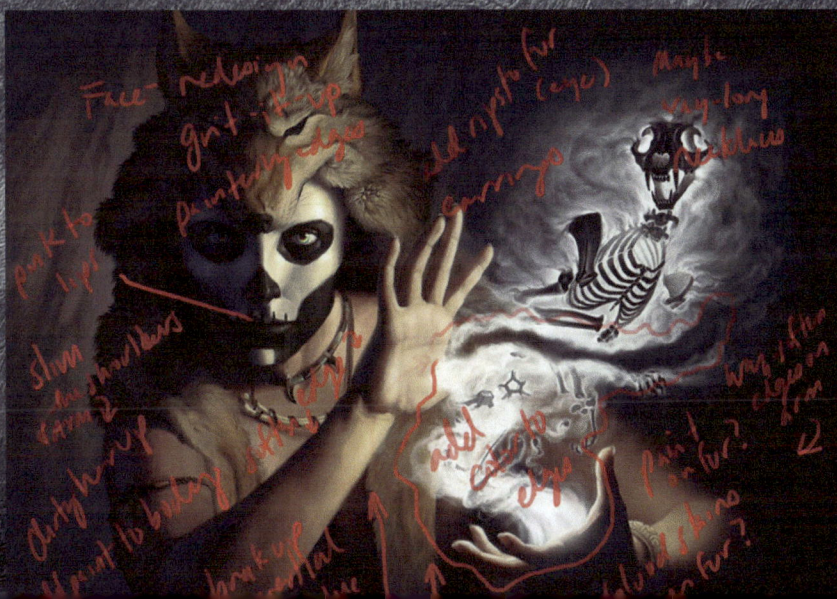

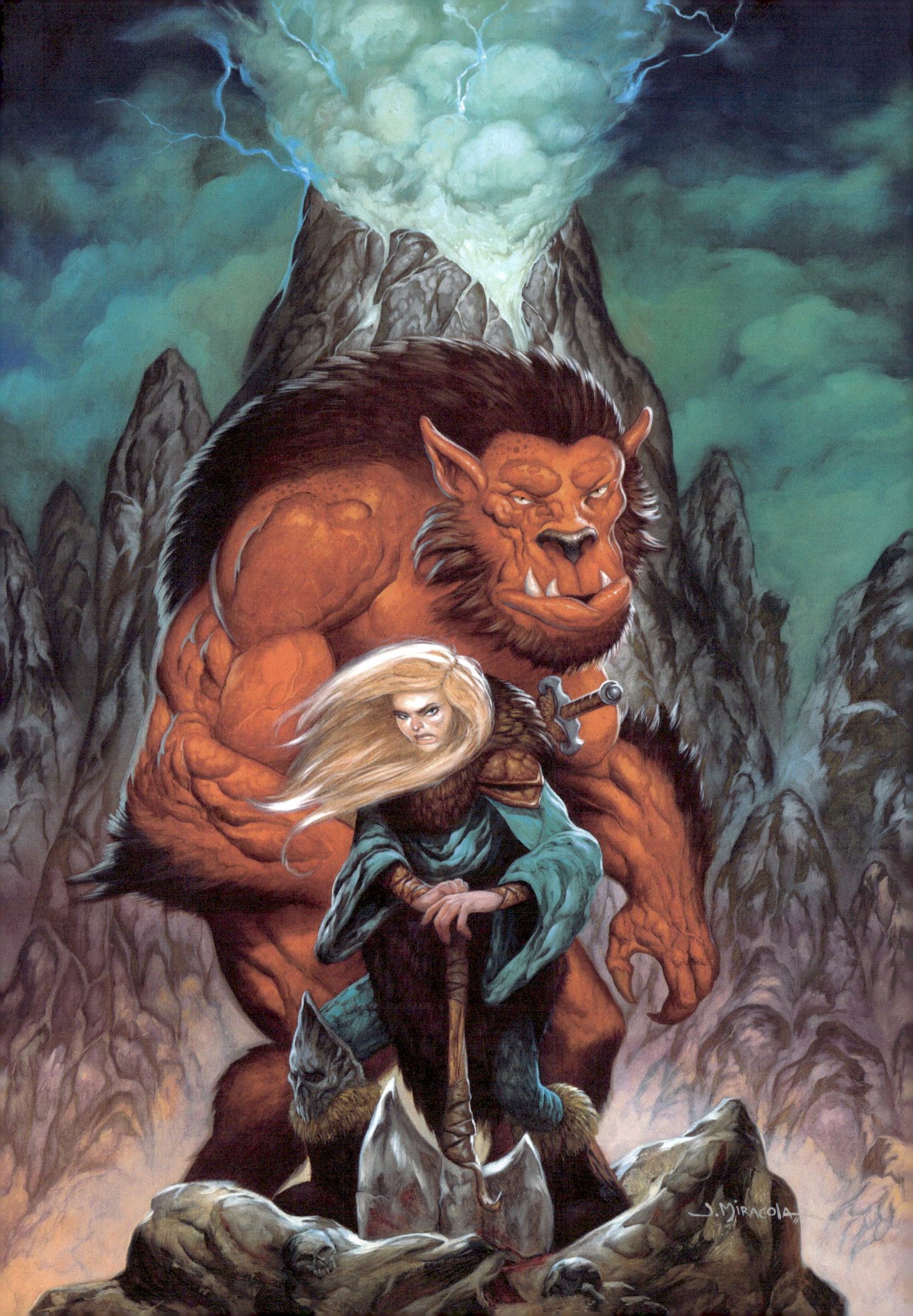

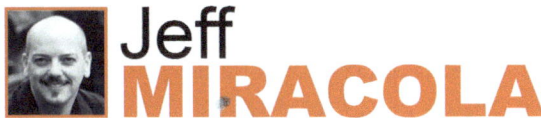

Jeff MIRACOLA

Website: www.jeffmiracola.com
Title: Forsaken
Art: Oil on masonite 16" x 24"

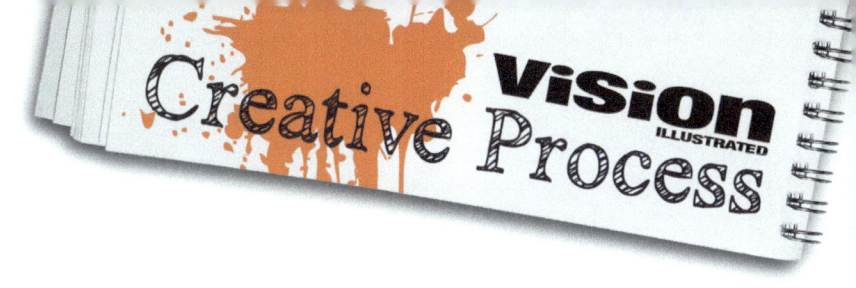
1 Thumbnail Sketches

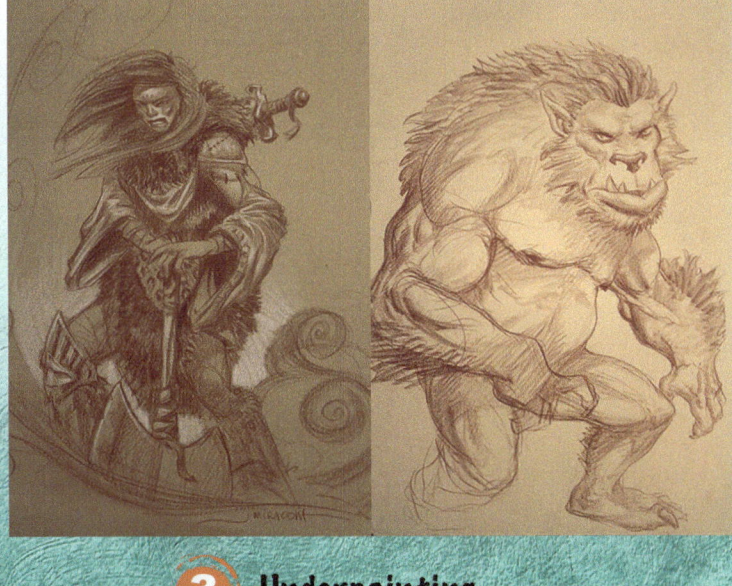

2 Transfer Sketch

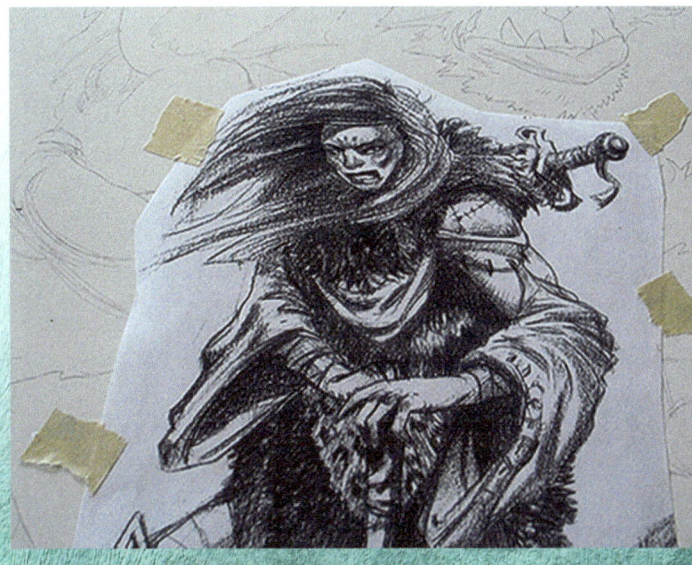

3 Underpainting

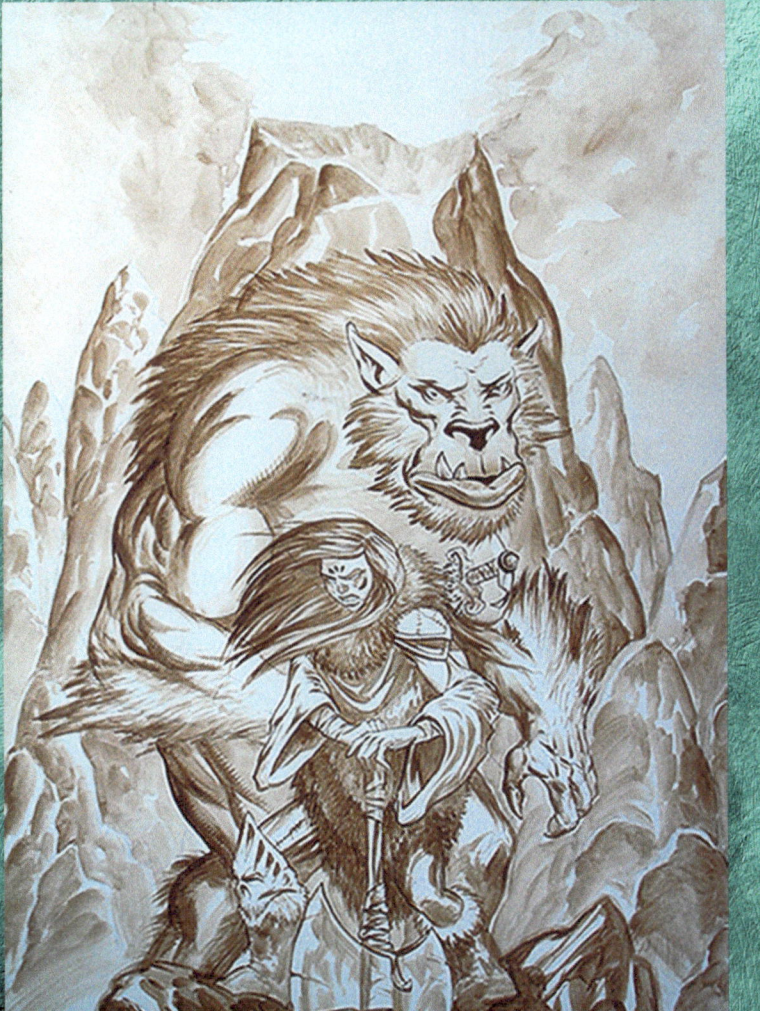

4 Progress Images

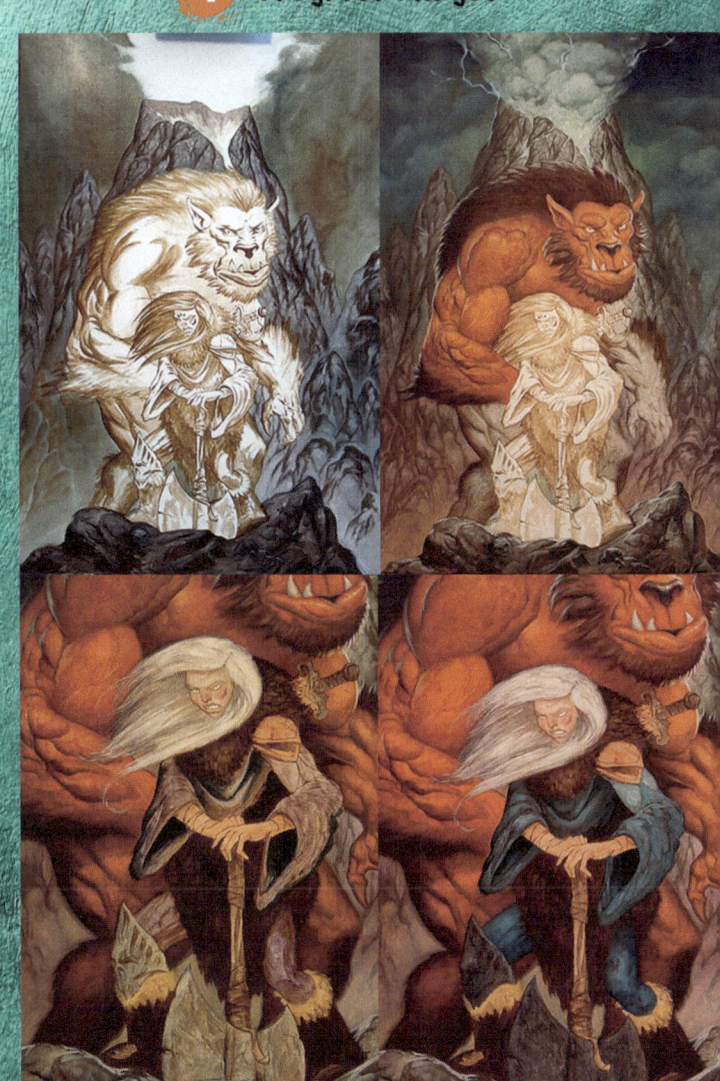

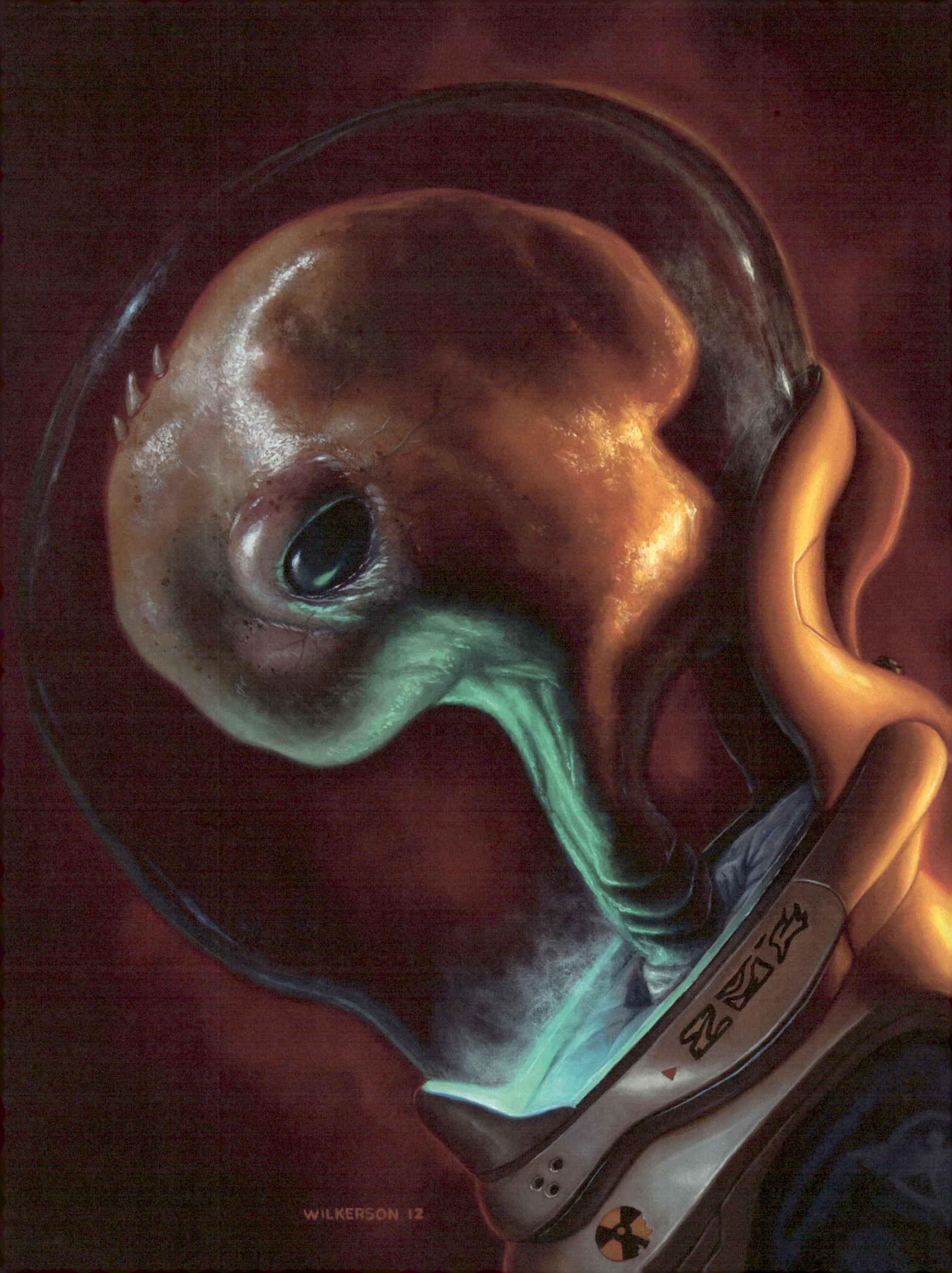

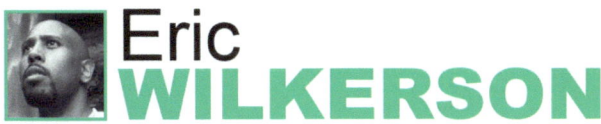

Eric
WILKERSON

Website: www.ericwilkersonart.com
Title: Kush
Art: Oil on panel 20" x 22"

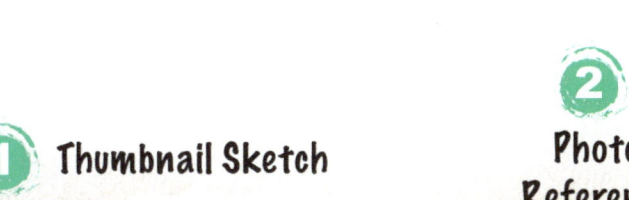
1 Thumbnail Sketch

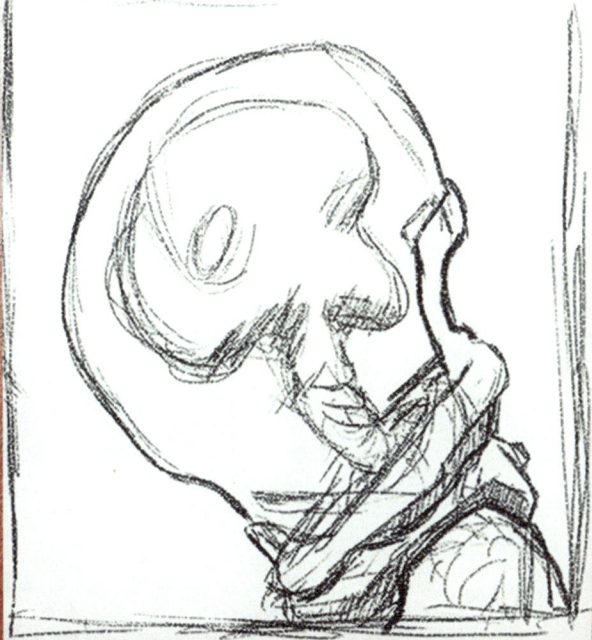

2 Photo Reference

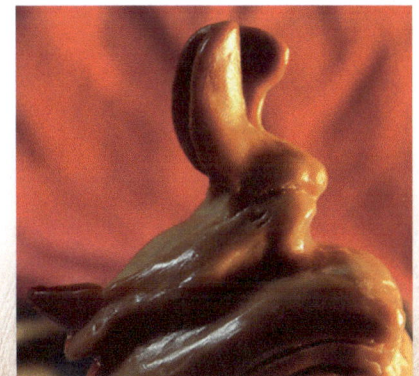

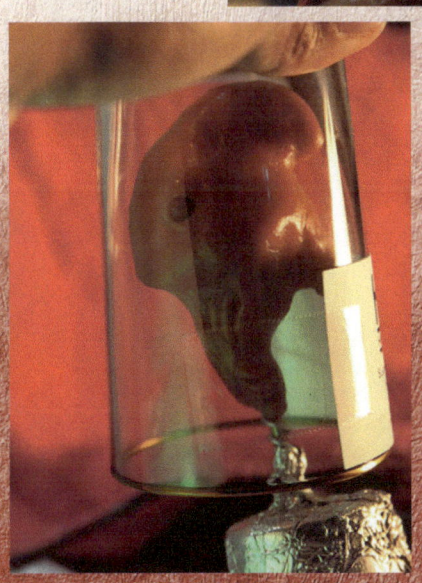 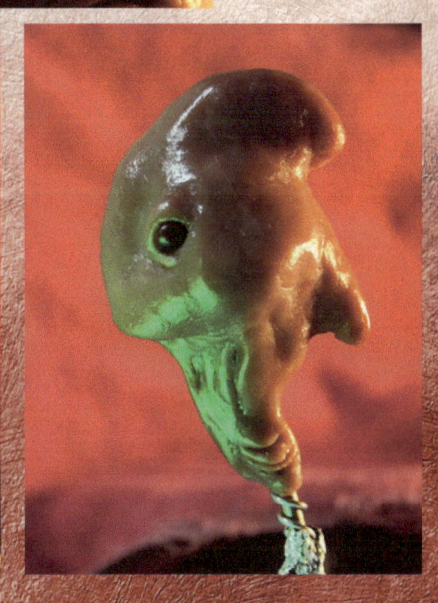

3 Color Study

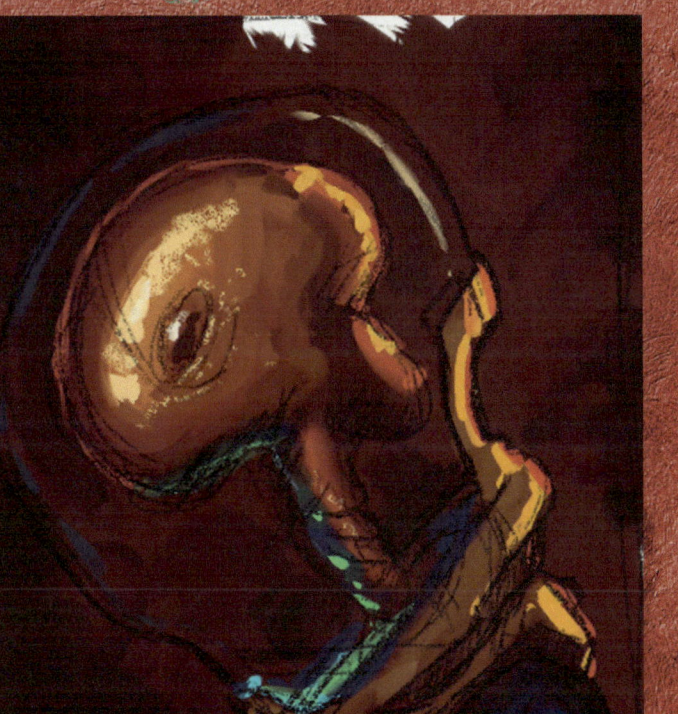

4 Final Drawing

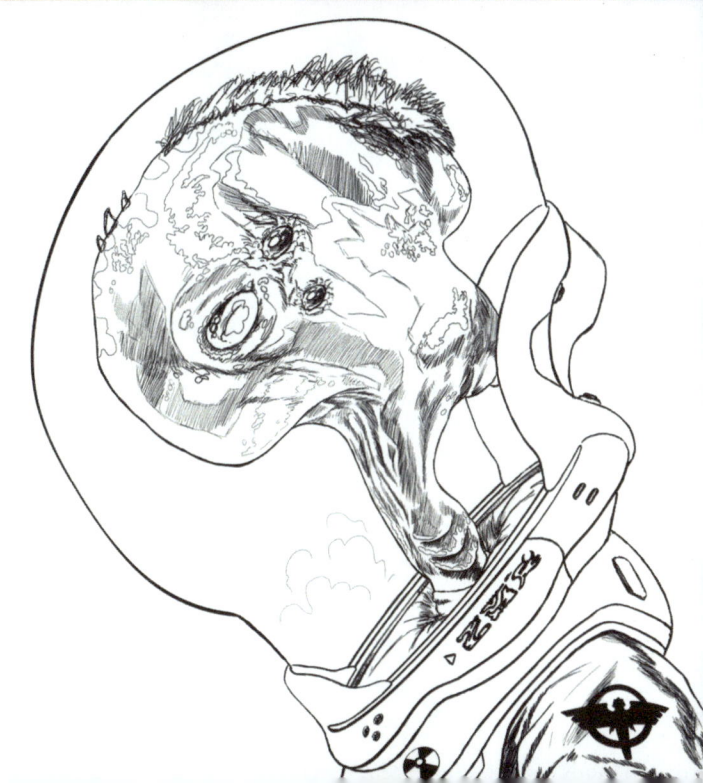

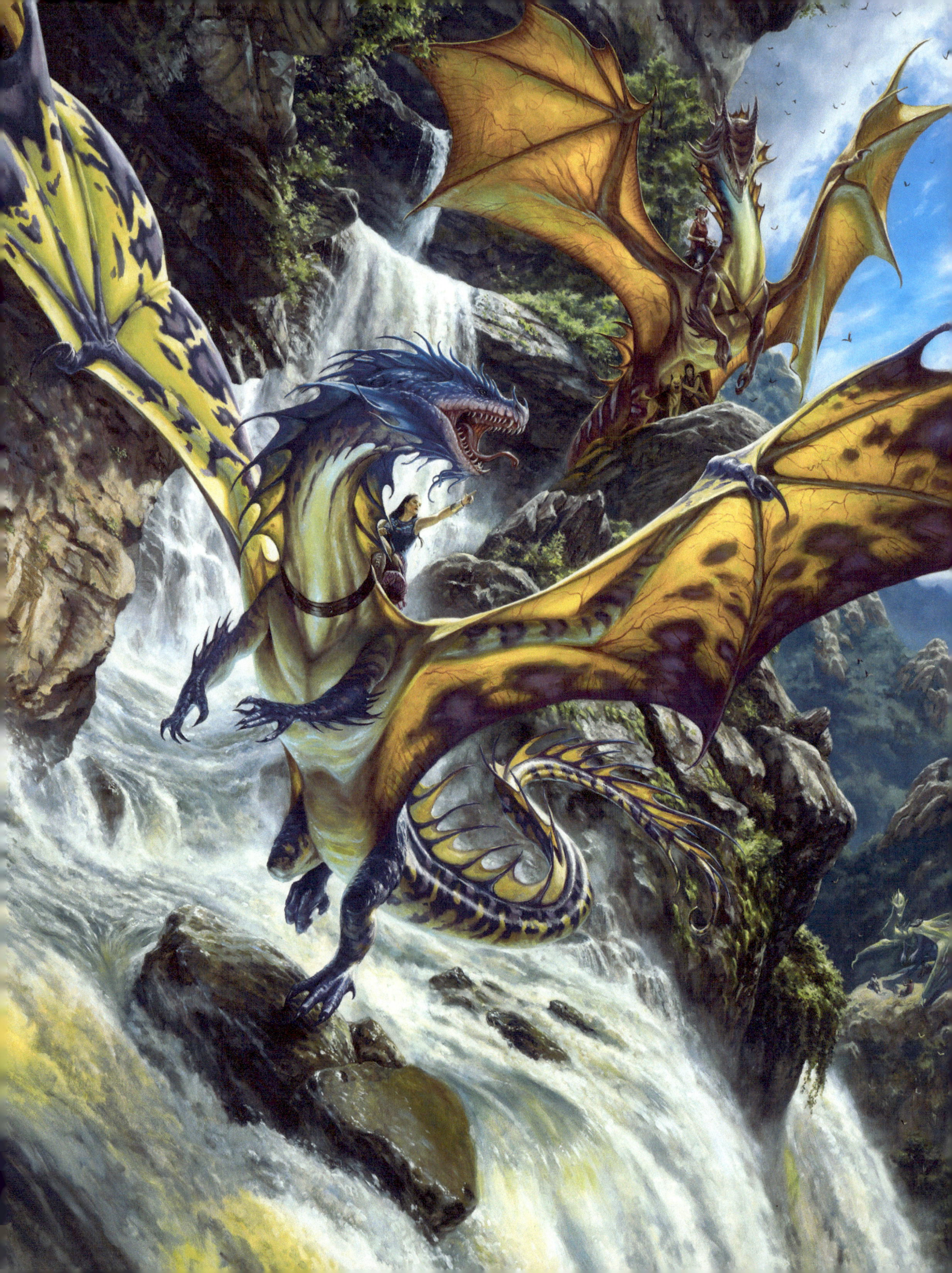

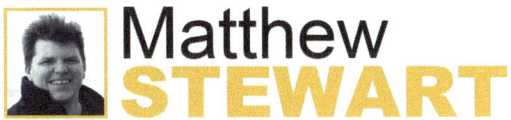

Matthew STEWART

Website: www.matthew-stewart.com
Email: matt@matthew-stewart.com
Title: Waterfall Dragons
Art: Oil on board 32" x 40"

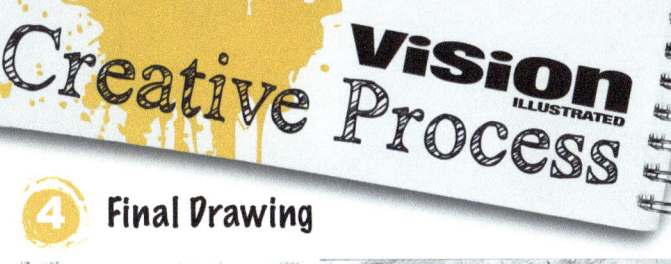

Creative Process

① Thumbnail Sketches

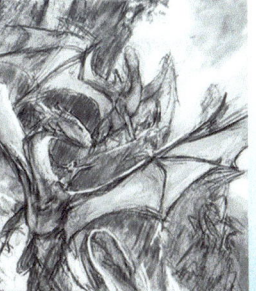

② Color Study

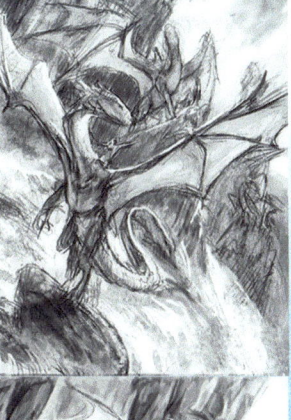

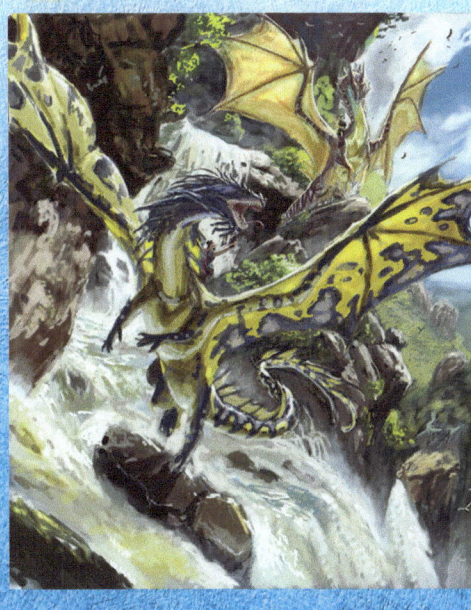

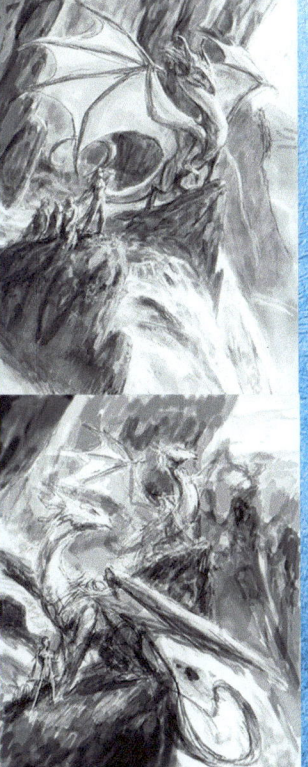

③ Photo Reference

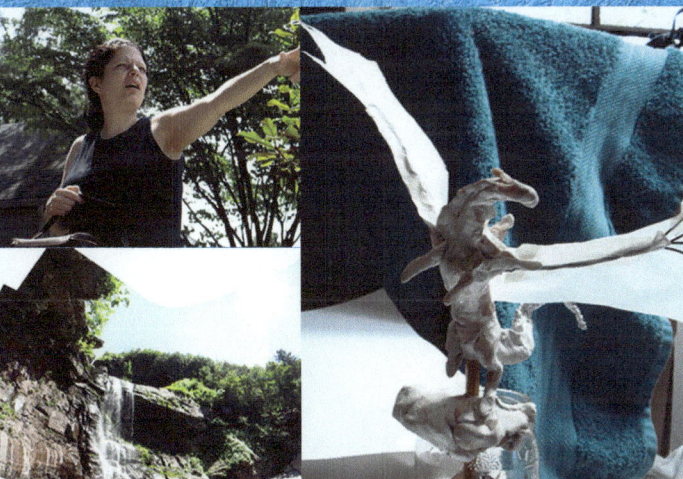

④ Final Drawing

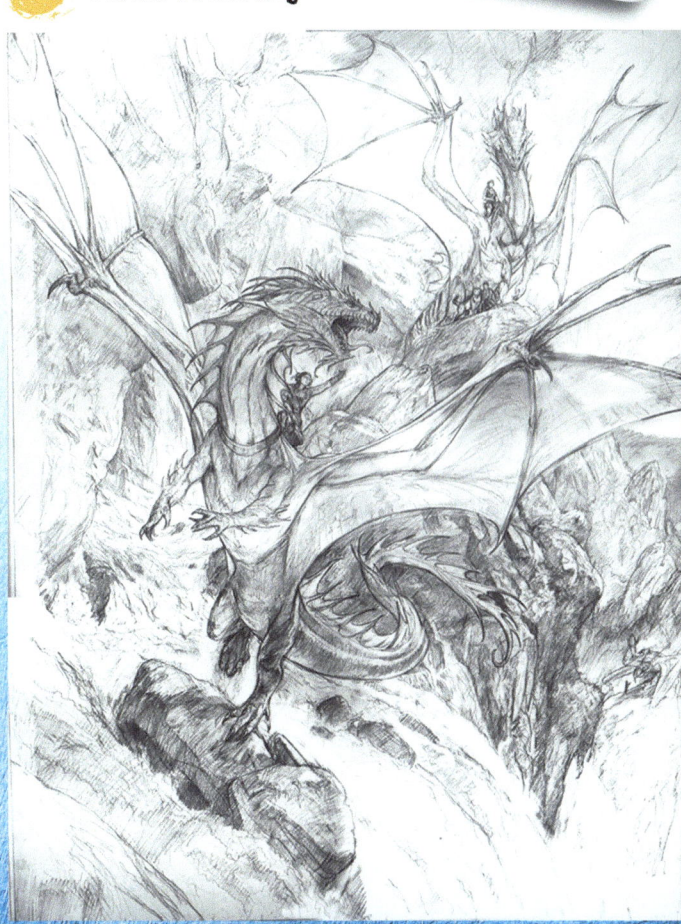

⑤ Progress Image

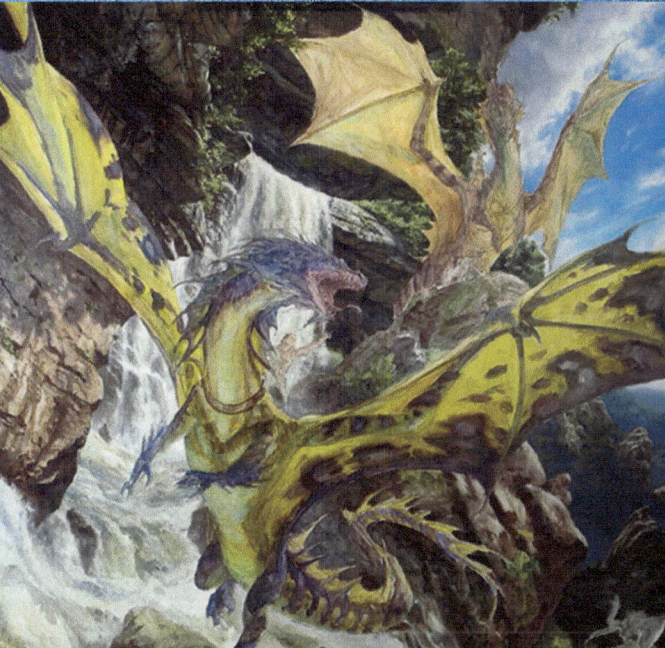

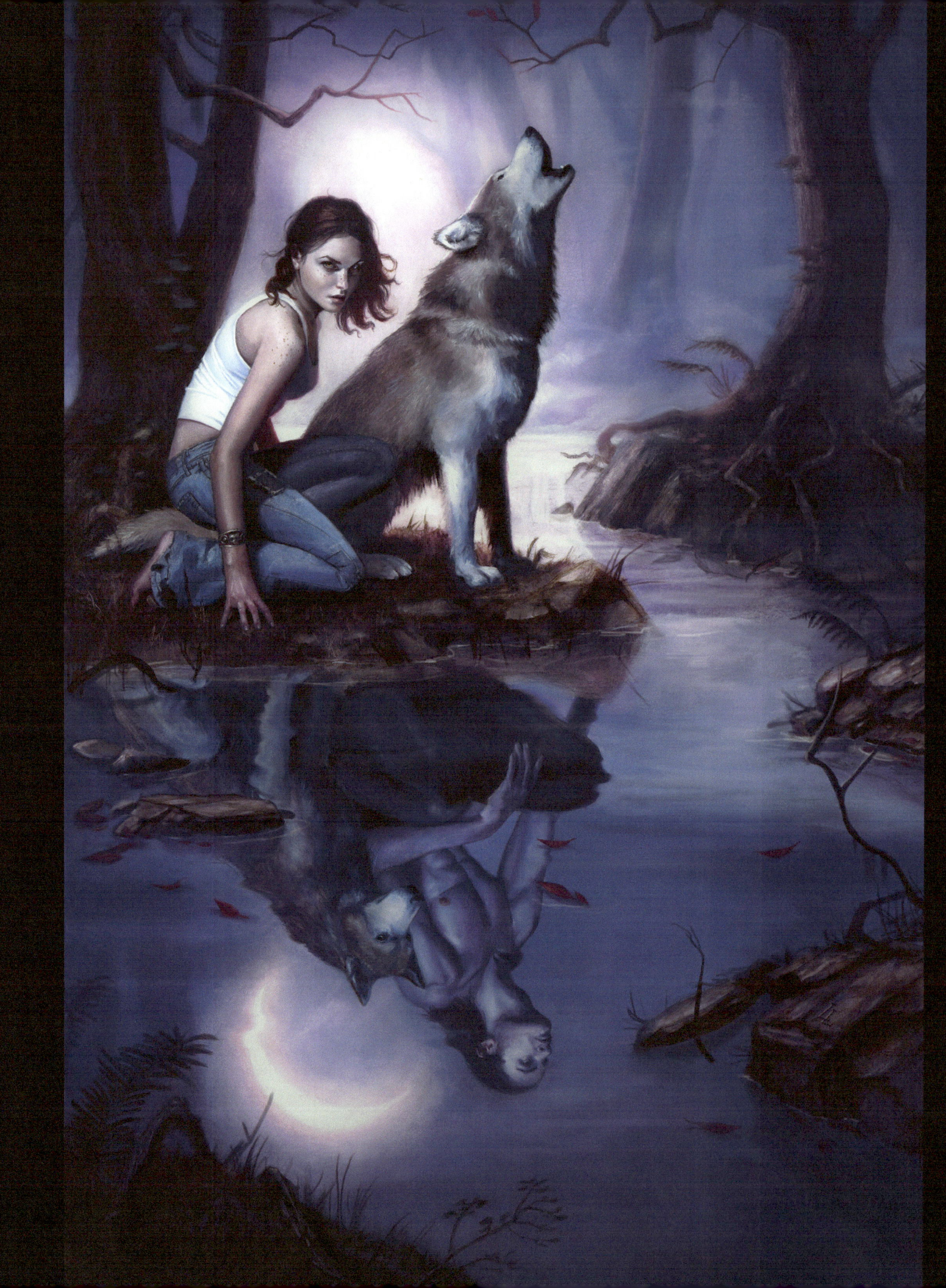

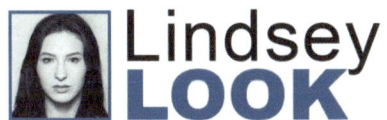

Lindsey LOOK

Website: www.lindseylook.com
Email: lindseylook@gmail.com
Title: Call of the Hunt
Art: Oil on board 18.5" x 28.5"

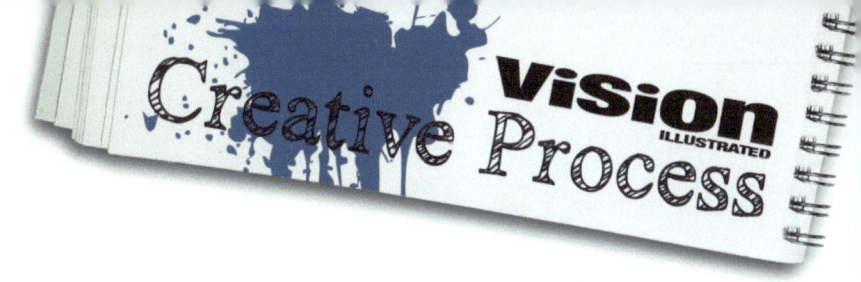

Creative Process — **viSiON** ILLUSTRATED

1 Thumbnail Sketches

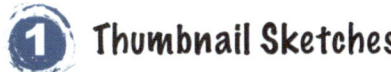

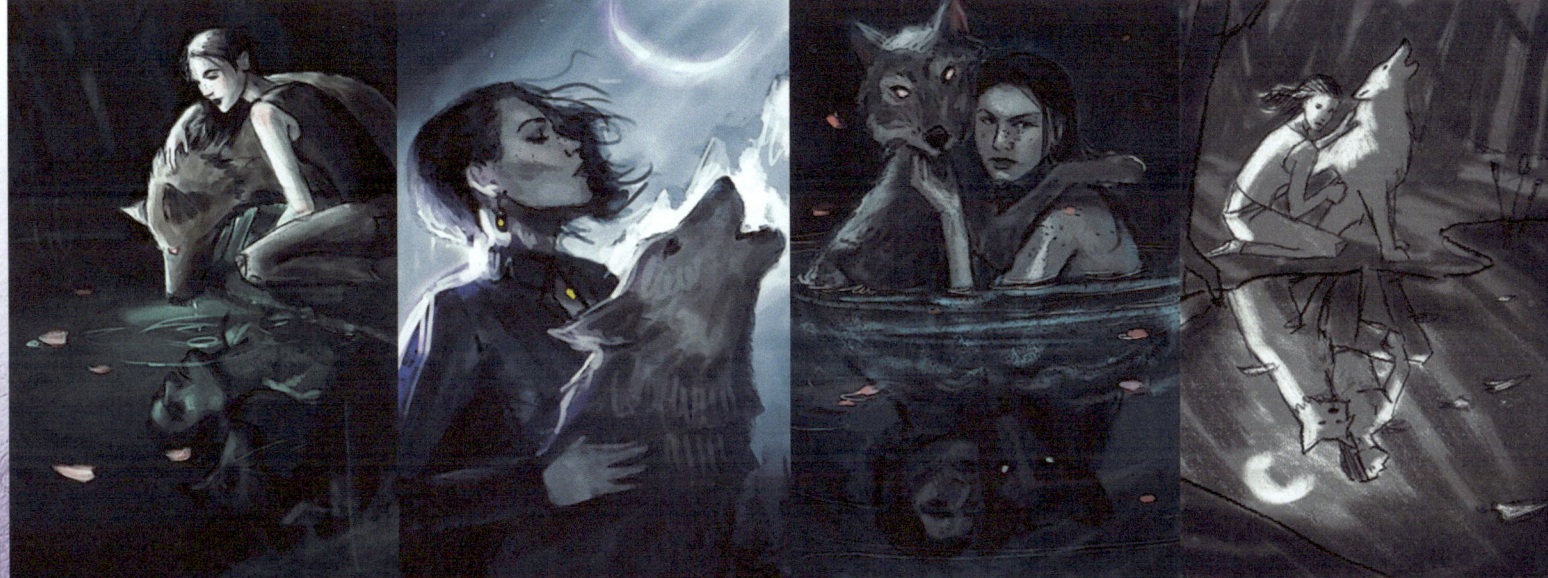

3 Progress Image

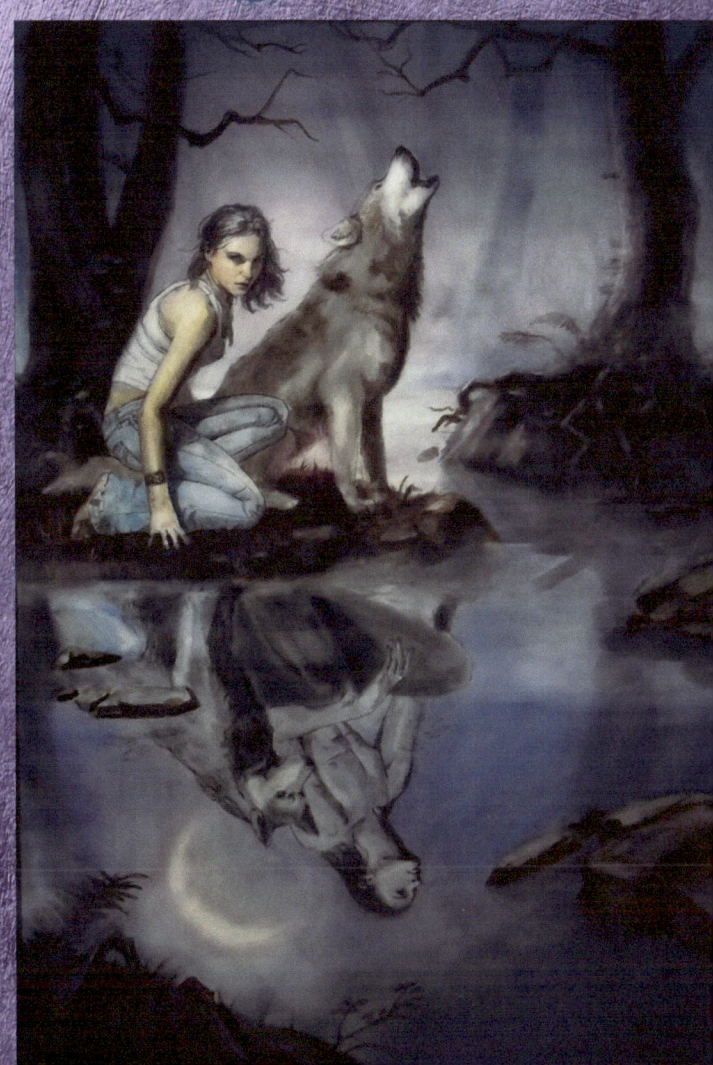

2 Photo Reference

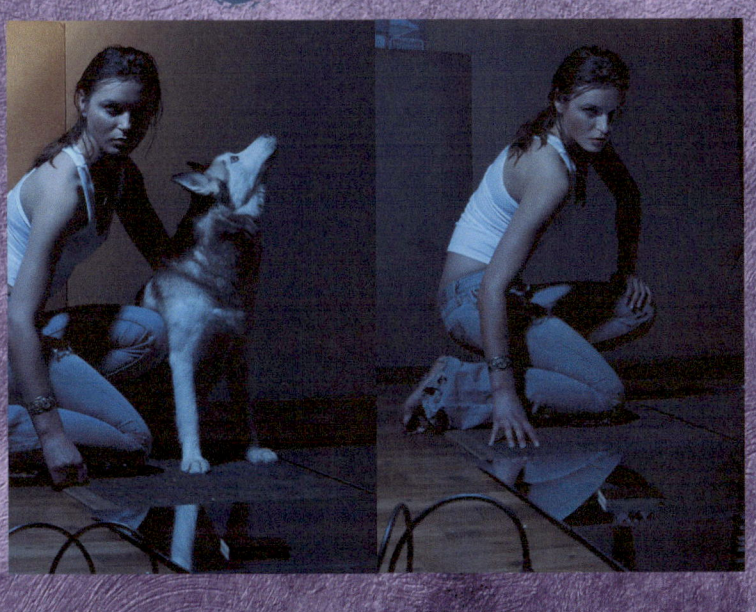

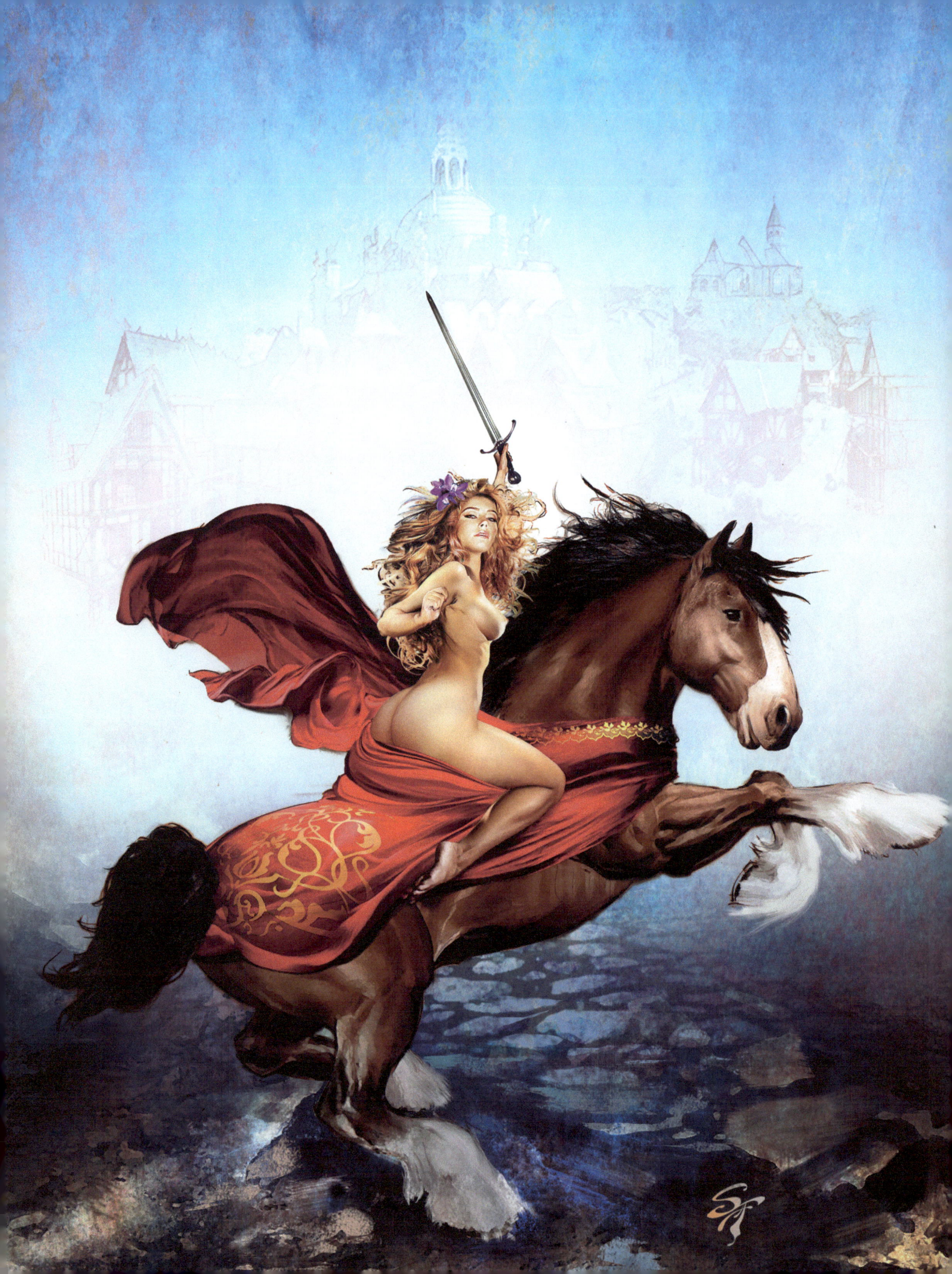

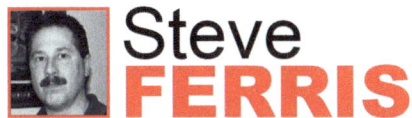

Steve FERRIS

Website: www.steveferris.com
Email: steveferris@optonline.net
Title: Godiva Bold
Art: Mixed media 26" x 20"

Creative Vision Process
ILLUSTRATED

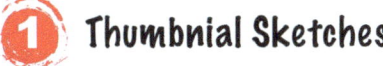

① Thumbnial Sketches

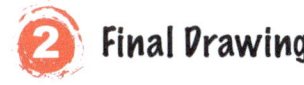

② Final Drawing

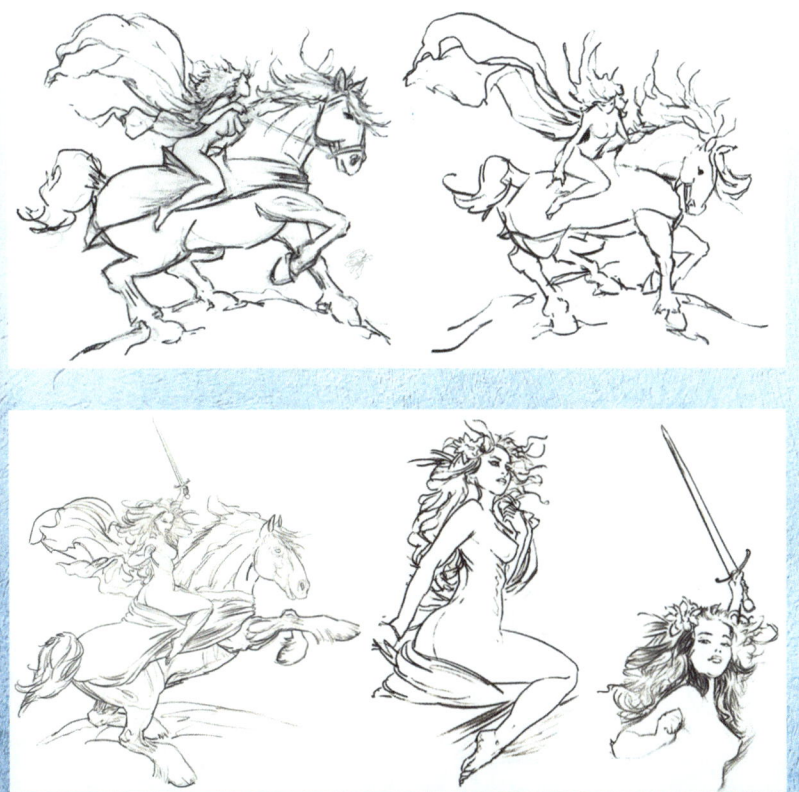

③ Progress Images

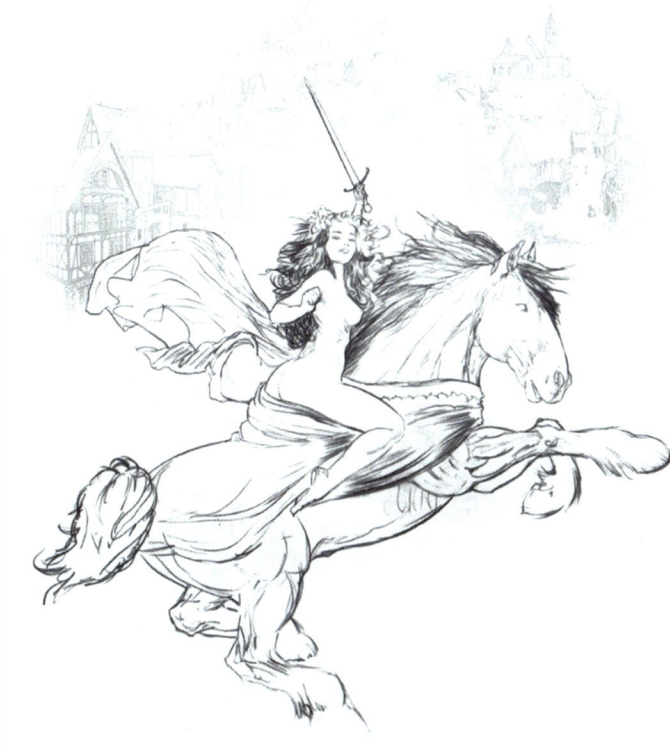

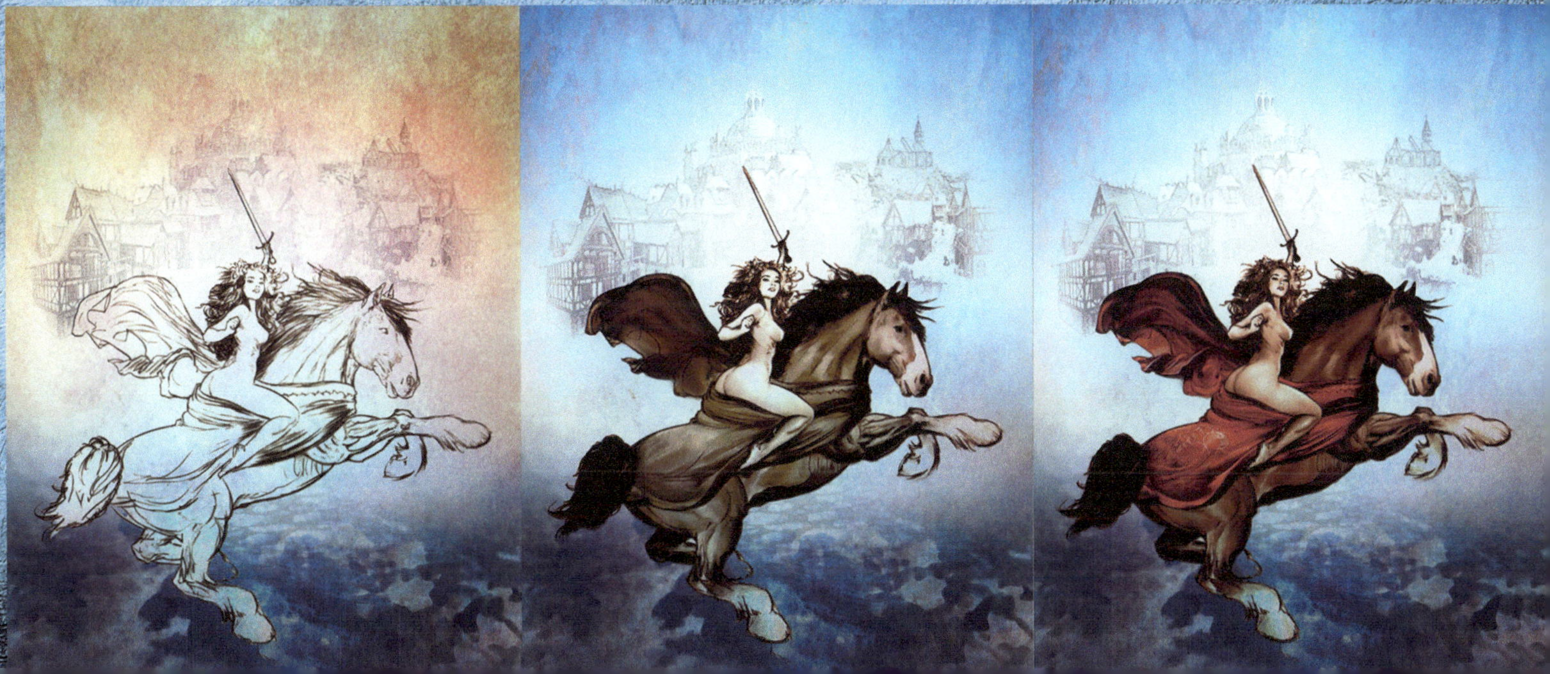

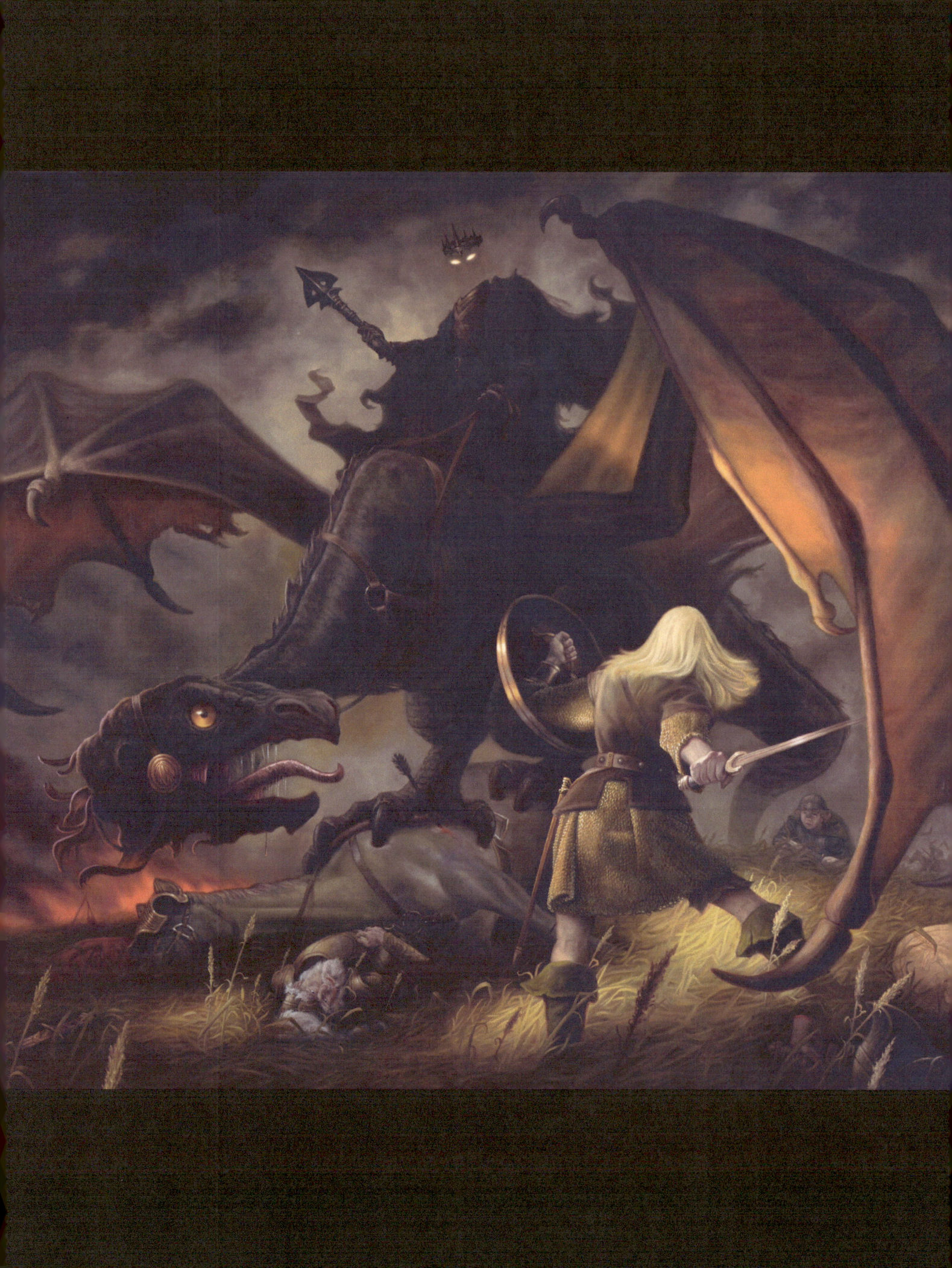

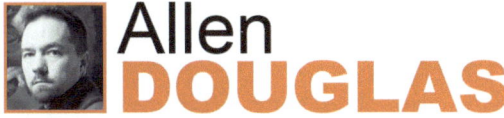

Allen DOUGLAS

Website: www.allendouglasstudio.com
Email: allen@allendouglasstudio.com
Title: Fields of Pelennor
Art: Oil on panel 48" x 44"

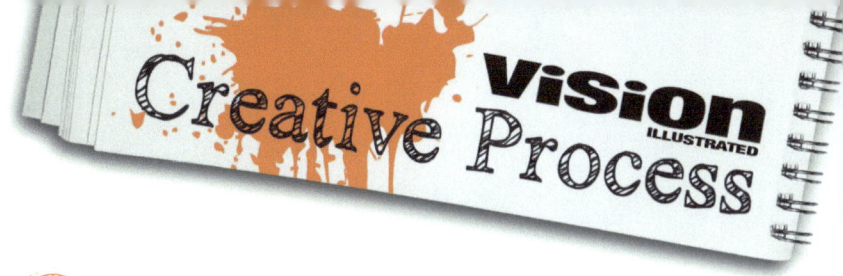

Creative Process

VISION ILLUSTRATED

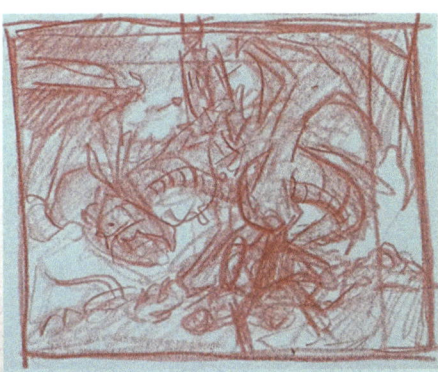

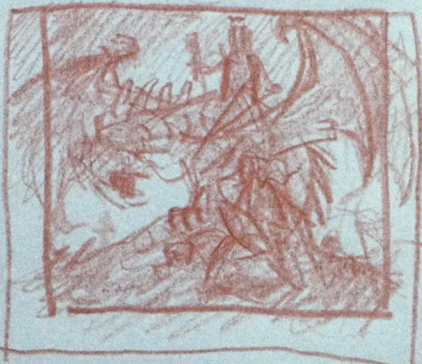

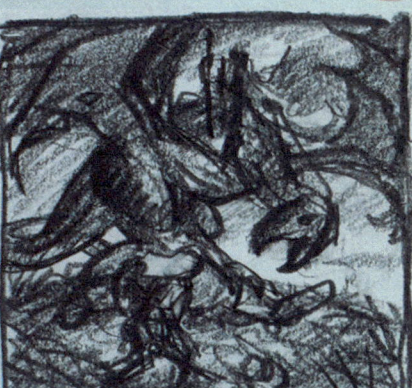

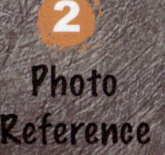
1
Thumbnail Sketches

2
Photo Reference

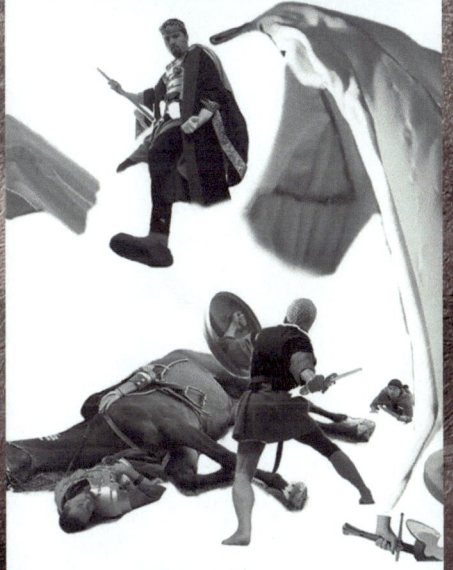

3 Color Study

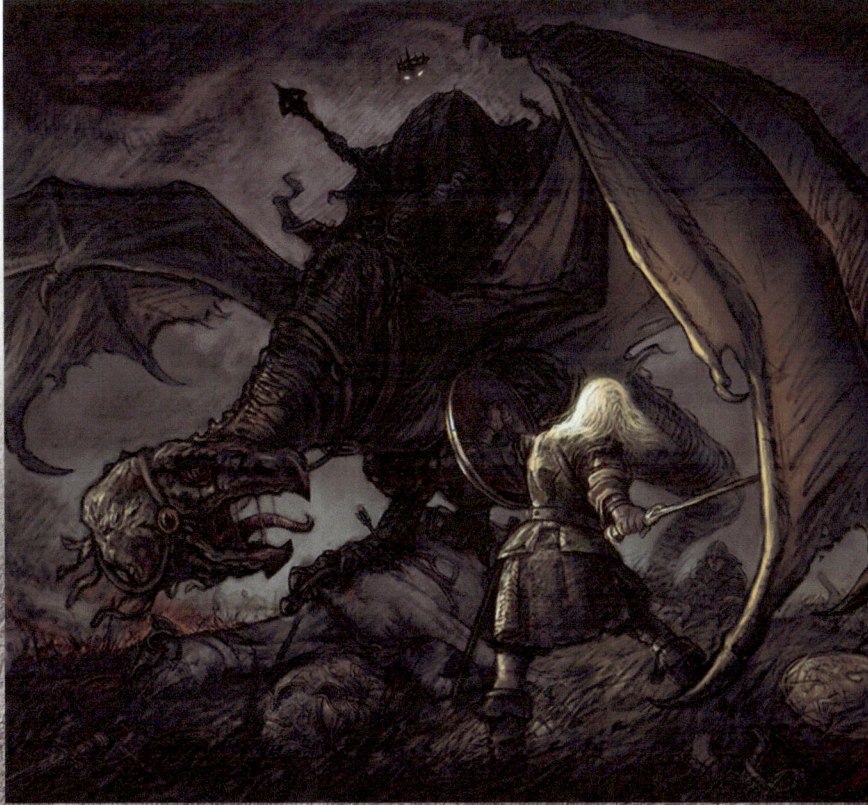

4 Final Drawing

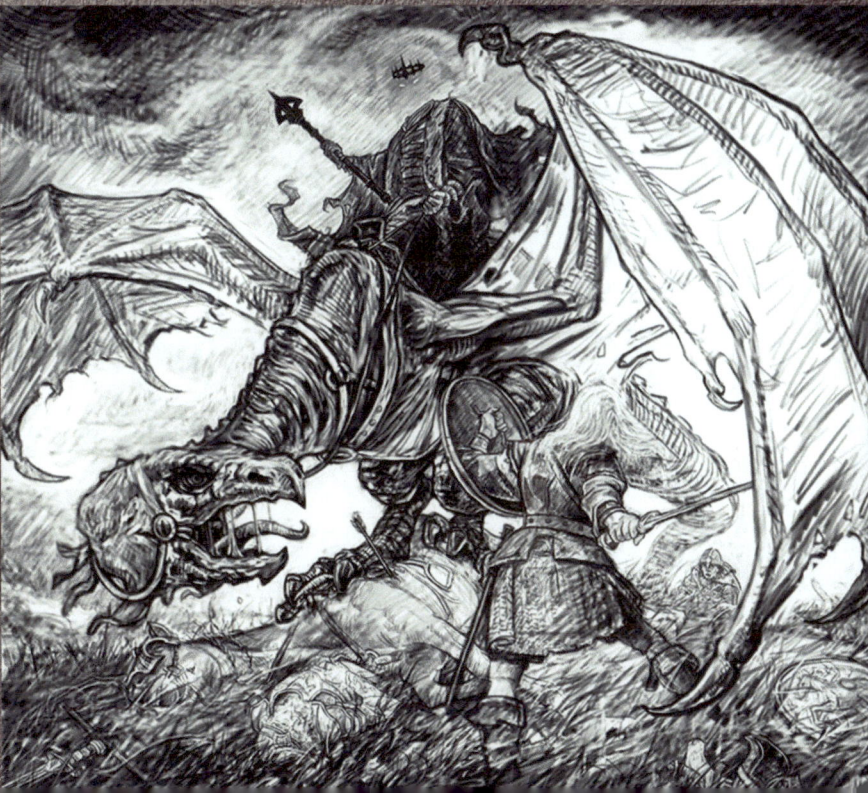

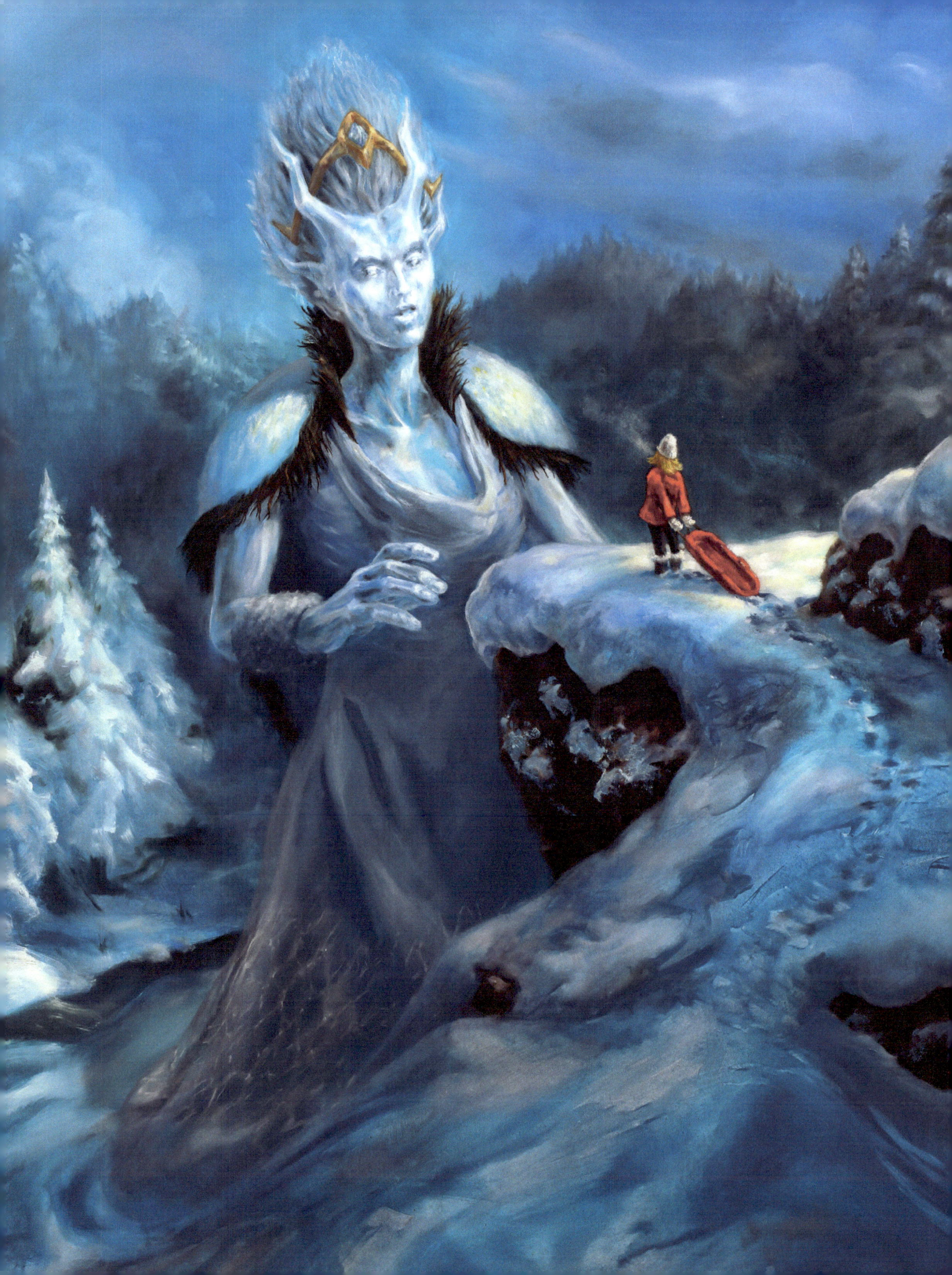

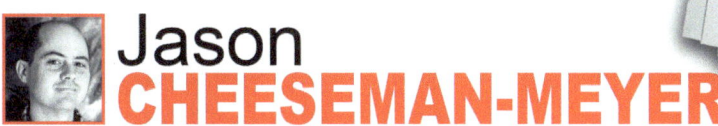

Jason
CHEESEMAN-MEYER

Website: www.cheeseman-meyer.com
Email: jasoncmeyer@gmail.com
Title: Winter's Daughter
Art: Oil on panel 24" x 36"

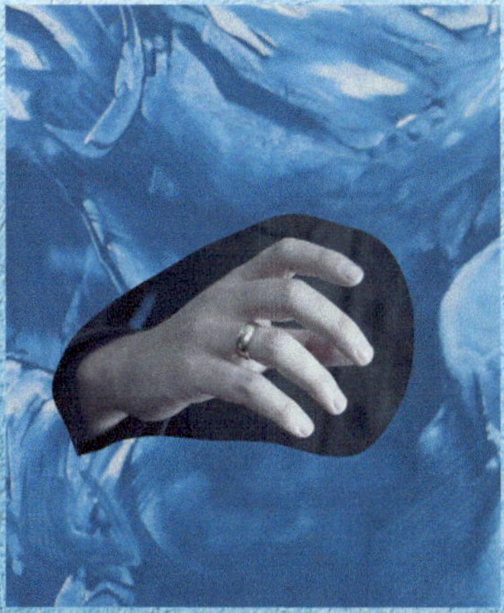

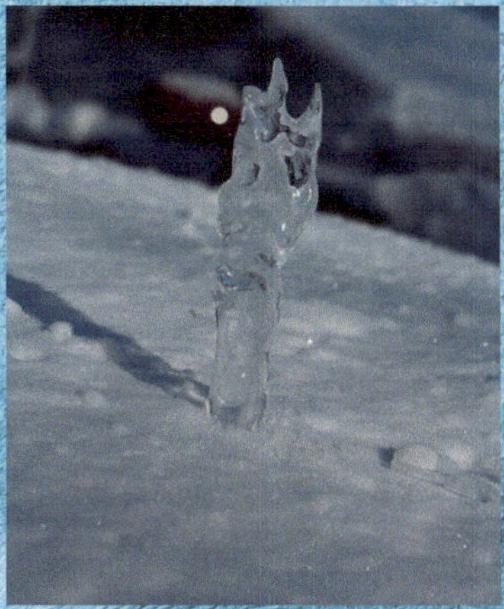

② **Progress Images**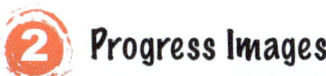

① **Photo Reference**

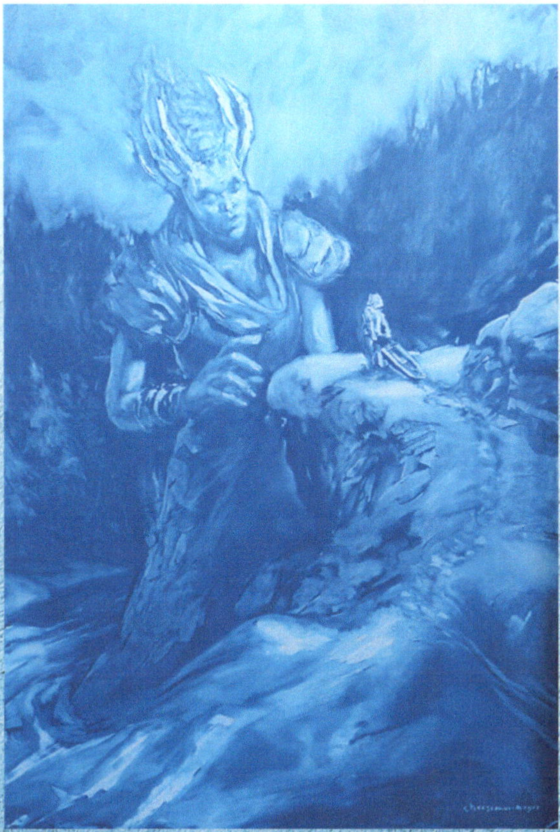

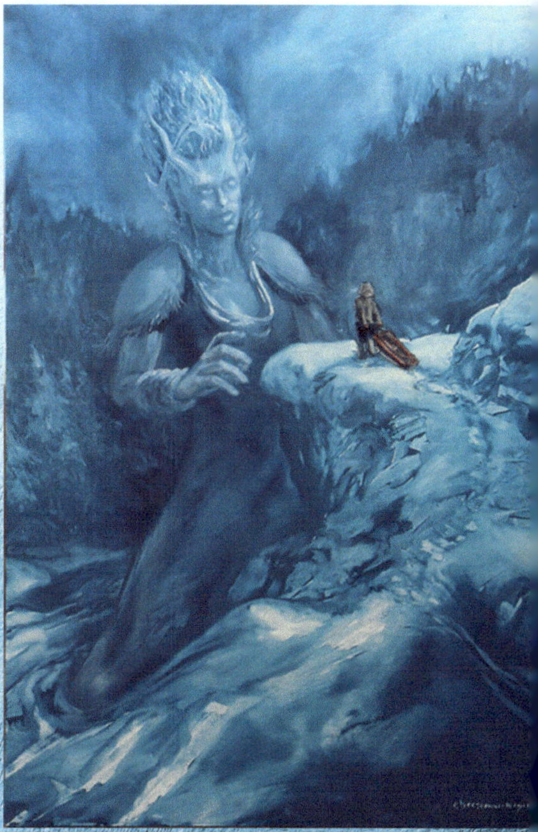

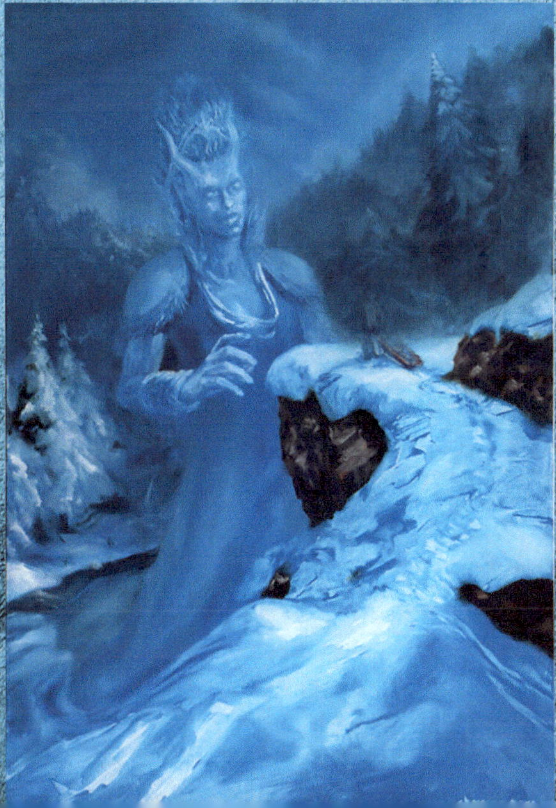

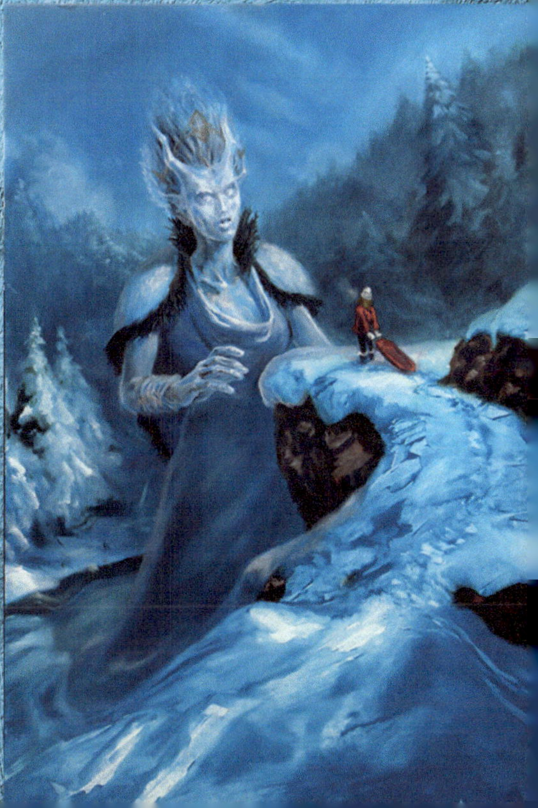

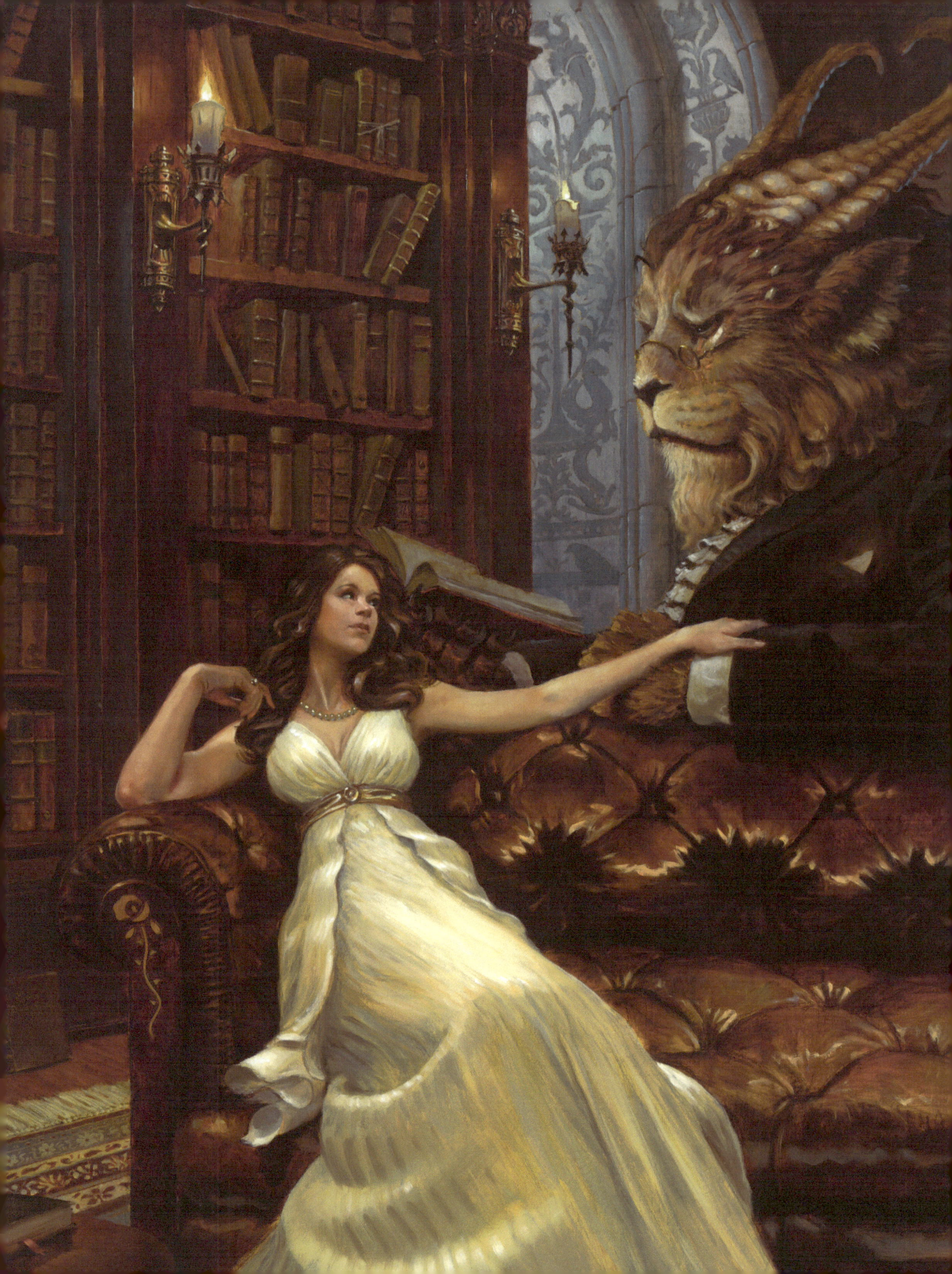

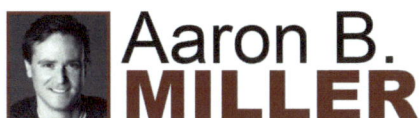

Aaron B. MILLER

Website: www.aaronbmiller.com
Title: Beauty and the Beast
Art: Oil on panel 24" x 32"

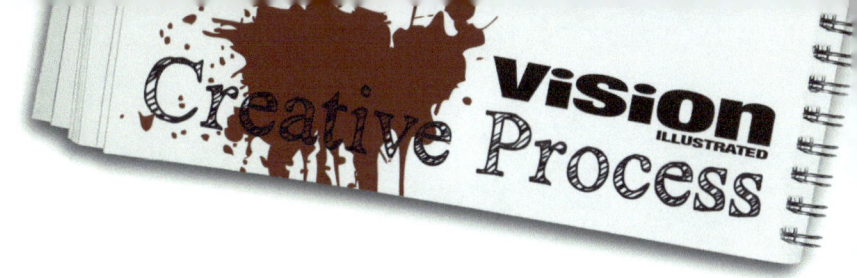
1 Thumbnail Sketch

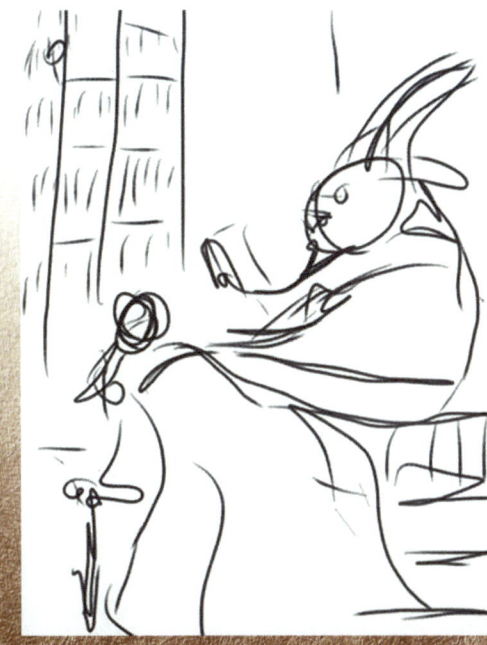

3 Black and White Study

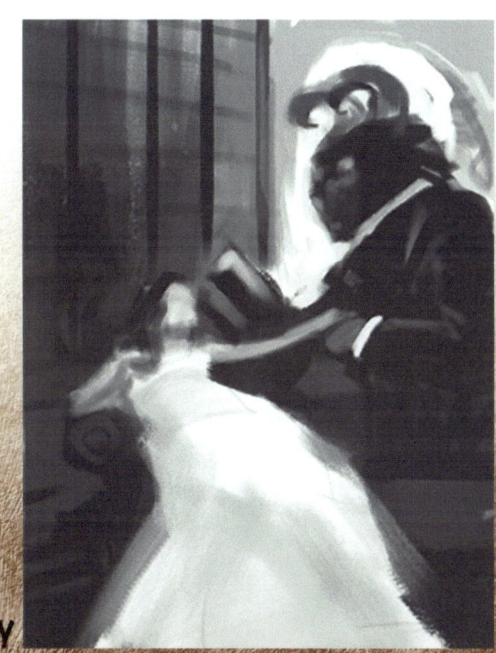

2 Preliminary Sketch

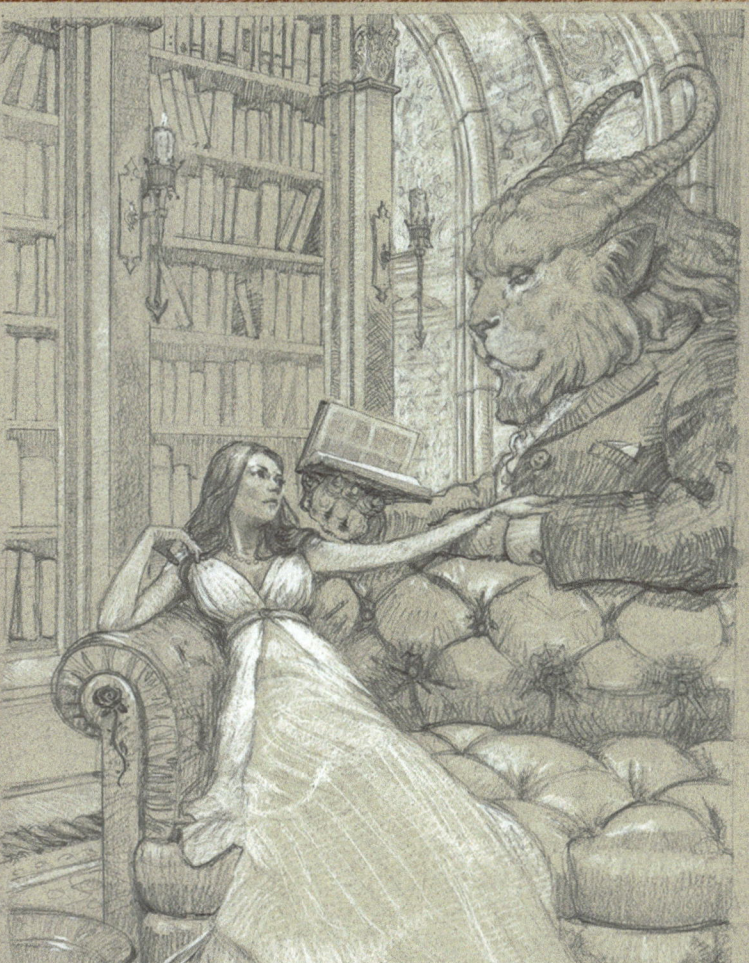

4 Final Drawing

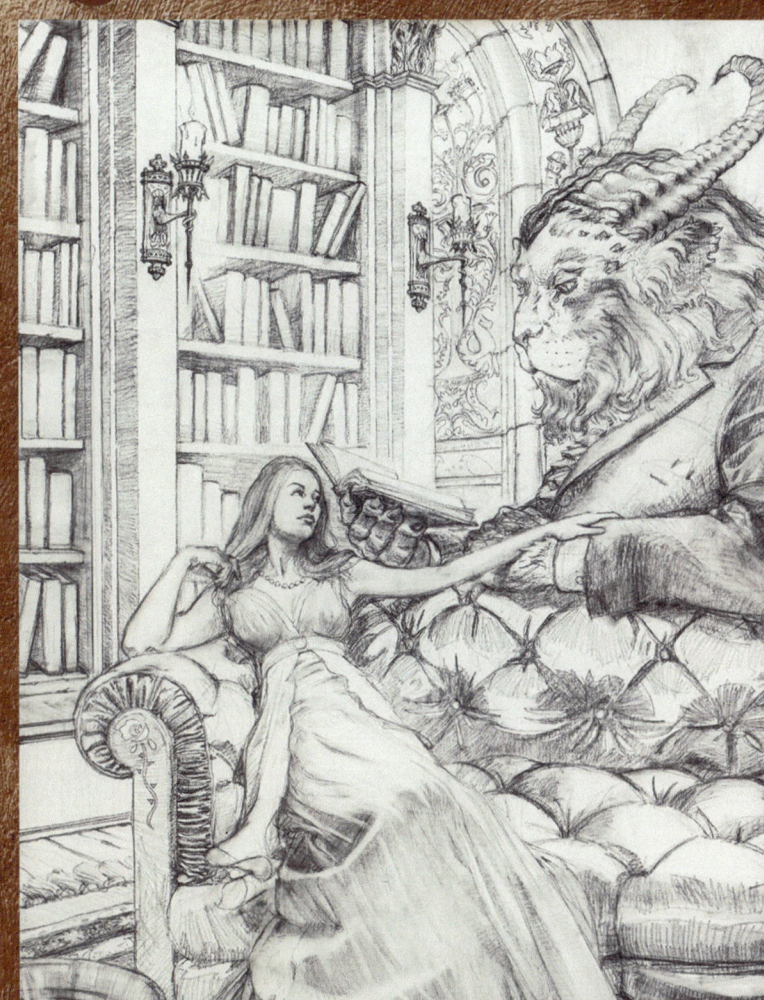

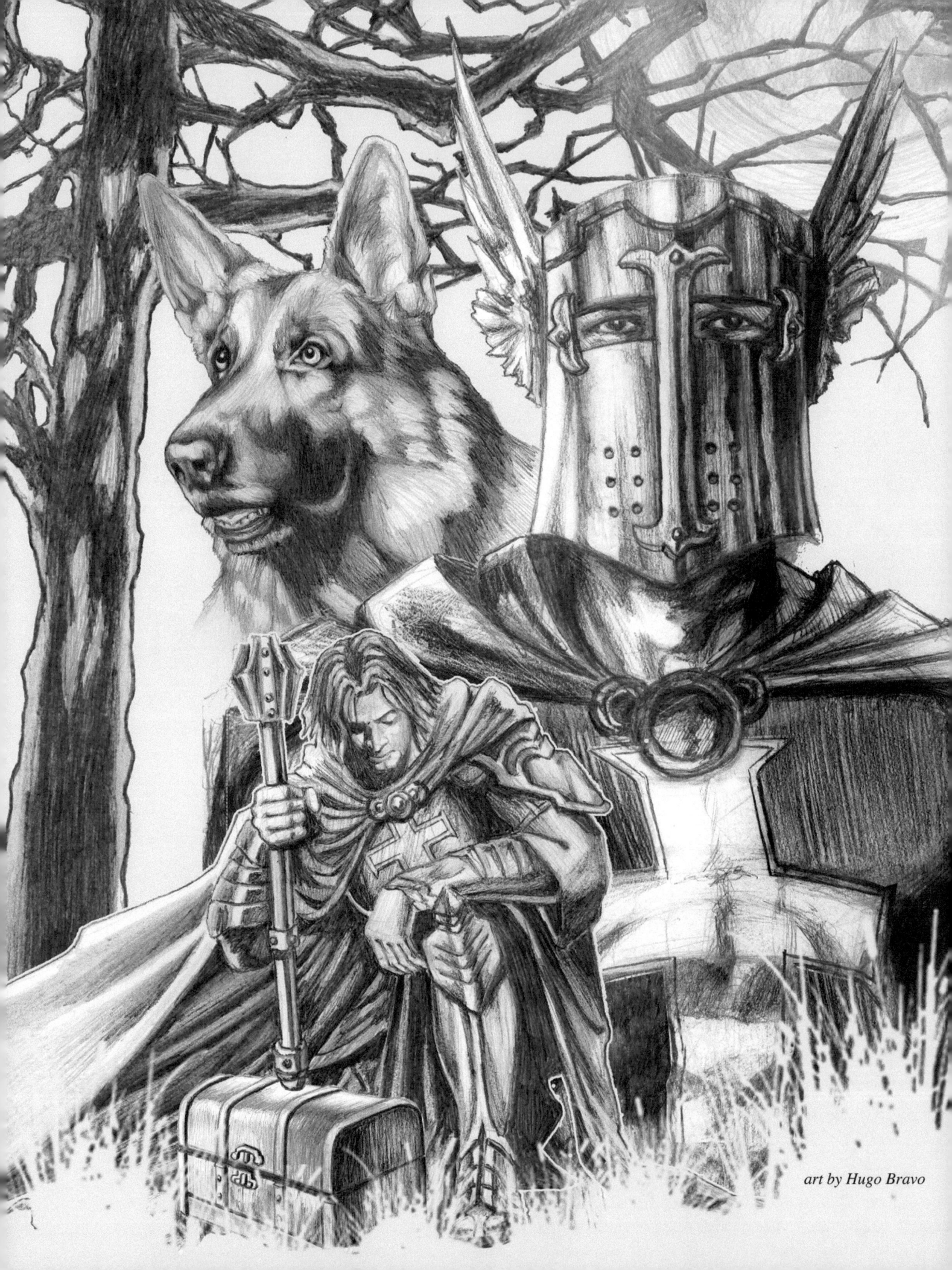

art by Hugo Bravo

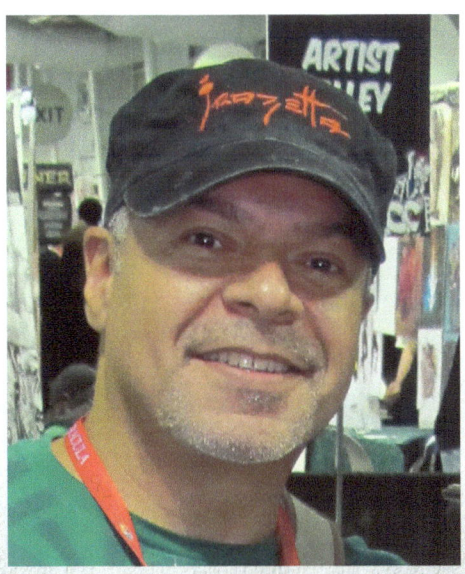

Thank You

The creation of a book of this magnitude is not taken lightly. I am thankful to all who helped along the way, starting with my muse MariLuz, who's faith in me and my art inspired me to take the journey of publishing my first book.

Big thanks to my great friend and illustrator Carlos Phoenix who provided his technical expertise and marketing ideas throughout the production of this book.

To Sal Lomedico, Albert Powell, Kevin Adams, Robert Luciano and other friends and colleagues who offered advice and feedback.

My eternal thanks to Donato Giancola who was the first artist I invited to be in the book and the first artist to believe in my book project.

To all the other artists who generously contributed art, without them this book would not exist.

To David Mammina who as a self published author advised me on all things related to self publishing.

Finally, I'd like to thank you the reader for buying this book to learn more about the artist's creative process.

Hugo Bravo

Hugo Bravo, Editor

Glossary

1 **Thumbnail Sketch**   Crude, small drawings used to develop the initial concept for a more detailed work.

2 **Black & White Study**   A rough drawing used to capture the toanl values of color used as the basis for a more detailed work.

3 **Color Study**   A drawing roughly colored used to capture the blance of color used as the basis for a more detailed work.

4 **Final Drawing**   A fully rendered drawing used as the foundation for producing the final work.

5 **Photo Reference**   Photographs used as a guide to realistically produce a work of art.

6 **Progress Images**   Photographs showing the stages of the art work being created.

7 **Transfer Sketch**   The use carbon paper, an opaque projector or other means to trace an image onto the surface of the final work.

8 **Underpainting**   The initial layer of paint used to establish tonal values in a painting, effectively painting a monochrome version of the final painting to get all the tonal values right before adding color.

www.ingramcontent.com/pod-product-compliance
Lightning Source LLC
Chambersburg PA
CBHW040744200526
45159CB00023B/1700